ONE MOVE
TO BETTER GOLF

ONE MOVE
TO BETTER GOLF

By CARL LOHREN with LARRY DENNIS

Introduction by DEANE BEMAN

Illustrations by ANTHONY RAVIELLI

A Golf Digest Book

Published by
Golf Digest, Inc.
A New York Times Company
297 Westport Avenue
Norwalk, Connecticut 06856

Quadrangle/
The New York Times Book Co.
10 East 53 Street
New York, New York 10022

First Printing
ISBN 0-8129-0558-X
LC 74-29499

TABLE OF CONTENTS

A DEDICATION *I dedicate this book to my wife Beryl who always has put my career in golf before her personal wishes. A golf professional could not have a better wife.*

ACKNOWLEDGEMENTS I want to express my gratitude to several persons who helped make this book possible.

First, my thanks go to Deane Beman, who first interested *Golf Digest* in this project and who helped me explain this method of swinging a golf club.

Secondly, I am in debt to Gene Borek, my long-time friend who is now the head professional at La Gorce C.C. in Miami, Fla. A respected teacher and fine player, Gene has embraced these concepts and has made great contributions to the text.

I am appreciative of the help I received from Irv Schloss, who helped me better define my thoughts related to this method, and to Dr. Alan Rosenthal, who aided me with research into the physiological aspects of how it works.

I would like to thank Jim Hundertmark, my assistant for nine years at North Shore C.C., who has been instrumental in helping me develop and test my ideas.

I thank Larry Dennis, who understands the complexities of the golf swing and has the ability to clearly transmit my thoughts into writing. And I appreciate the work done in editing this book by Cal Brown and the other editors of *Golf Digest.*

Last, but certainly not least, I want to thank Tony Ravielli, a superb artist whose special ability in illustrating this book has added immeasurably to its value.—*Carl Lohren*

INTRO-DUCTION

A motel room discussion with Carl Lohren during the 1968 Jacksonville Open changed my concept of how golf is played. Had it not been for that talk, I probably still would not know how all the parts of the golf swing fall into place.

I was in my second year as a professional after a satisfying amateur career. I had just finished second in a playoff at the Bob Hope Desert Classic, and I had a lot of confidence. By any reasonable measure, I was a successful player.

I also thought I had a lot of knowledge of the golf swing. I had spent a great deal of time thinking about it and practicing. But in retrospect I was the product of 50 years of teaching the unrelated parts of the swing, and I was hung up on them. I was always looking for gimmicks, something that would give me the secret.

Carl Lohren was a college classmate and long-standing friend, but that was not the reason I accepted his system. I had enough knowledge to recognize that what Carl was telling me was right. He gave me a road map, a structure, a framework for the golf swing. In the future it would prevent me from going up the blind alleys we all travel in searching for the secret to an effective, repeating golf swing. That was the significance of the system which Carl outlined for me, and it is the significance of this book.

Most people who learn golf do so in a disjointed, piecemeal manner. Too seldom has the golfer been made to realize that everything he does in the golf swing must fit into a structure which helps him build an effective swing. This book tells us why and how every component of the golf swing is interrelated. Thus, it is a systematic approach rather than a collection of uncoordinated facts.

This book relates to your primary goal of striking a golf shot in the most effective manner, and it tells you how to accomplish it. It will appeal to an intelligent, organized mind because it provides something you can believe in.

When you have something to believe in, a couple of things happen. First, that belief will in itself lower your anxiety level and help you perform better. Secondly, it will enable you to know what you have to do to produce the kind of shot you need so that you can focus your mind on that. This breeds a great deal of confidence because you know where you are going and how you are going to get there.

The human mind is a goal-seeking mechanism. It will respond to an objective, but if it tries to deal with unrelated parts that conflict with each other, it can't properly and consistently seek that goal. Lohren's system provides a clear, identifiable way to achieve specific goals in your golf swing. His concept becomes simple and logical because it is properly structured. The mind can handle it. It is built around basic precepts that are easily recalled.

A golf swing that is built on total muscle memory—as I had tried to build mine—is subject to the ups and downs of your emotional makeup and the problems of the hour. That kind of swing depends on your ability to block out interference and leave the mind blank so that your muscle memory can work. Try not to think about what you are not supposed to think about. That's very difficult for the mind to deal with. It can easily be directed toward a specific thought or goal, a triggering action, but it cannot deal so readily with fending off bad thoughts.

On the other hand, a well-reasoned, simple system that you can call on in times of stress makes your swing stronger under pressure.

When you are playing, the mind has a difficult time focusing on more than one thing. It can focus on a positive or a negative thought. Before Carl's concept was presented to me, when I came down the stretch in a golf tournament, all kinds of things would go through my mind. I would be focusing on results—I had to make a birdie on this hole, or knock a 2-iron shot to within 10 feet of the hole to win—instead of focusing on what I needed to do to get those results. I'm sure you have found yourself in the same position in a club tournament or even when the Sunday bet was riding on the last hole. Knowing Lohren's system and having confidence in his starting move invariably helped me to produce a good golf shot in circumstances like these because I could depend on the move to work.

This book is not telling you how Carl Lohren plays or how Deane Beman plays. Carl is saying that this is what the great swingers do and what you can do to play better.

Some will read this book and conclude that the movement of the left shoulder is the secret. Obviously that is of paramount importance because that is where it all starts. But to me the secret of the book is the system, a precise and logical approach to the golf swing that puts all of the golf-swing fundamentals in clear and proper perspective.

The book defines the conflict between right and left. Understanding that conflict is the basis of left-side control, and if you don't accept that, you don't accept the modern golf swing.

Lohren's system explains the fundamentals that enable the left side to win the battle. It gives you a way to start your golf swing so that nothing in that swing opposes those fundamentals. This brings a structure to the golf swing. At the same time it allows leeway for a golfer's personal mannerisms and physical traits.

There is nothing magical about this system. I have been using it for seven years now, and I am still learning. It will have an immediate beneficial effect on your golf swing. Naturally, to keep improving you must work at this as at anything else worthwhile. After you have read this book, I think you will be willing to work. People tend to seek the easy way—a shortcut, a gimmick—unless they can be convinced there is a sure way. Once they are given a reasoned, integrated system and have full knowledge of it, they will put effort into making it work.

The concept contained in this book will enable the low-handicap golfer to clear his mind of less important mechanics and to focus on the controlling factors of the swing. It will allow him to relate his natural instincts and talent to the physical principles that work in the golf swing. It will orient him to his objective, the total, interrelated golf swing, in a way that he has never been before.

The high-handicapper will be able to start thinking in broader terms than individual movements of the hips or arms or legs. He will learn to connect everything he does. He will make greater and faster improvement because he will go down fewer wrong paths. He will always be able to test any change he tries to make in his swing against that over-all structure. He will be able to discard a lot of gimmicks before he wastes time on them.

The depth of knowledge of the golf swing contained in this book is much greater and more explicit than I have seen presented before. It is laid out in such a clear-cut, logical way that, in my opinion, it will be the cornerstone of golf instruction for the foreseeable future.

DEANE R. BEMAN
Commissioner, Tournament Players Division
Professional Golfers Ass'n of America

PREFACE: HOW HOGAN'S SWING LED ME TO THE MOVE

I had searched a long time for a better way to strike the golf ball. I had been playing competitive golf since I was 11 (1949) and had turned professional in 1961, but I wasn't satisfied with the way I hit the ball. For example, my drives would upshoot, starting low and zooming high. I knew I had to get the ball out there on a lower trajectory with more roll. I had the feeling that the way to do this was to keep the clubhead on the ball longer through the impact area, but I didn't know how.

Ben Hogan rescued me, although of course he never knew it. I began watching him in 1957 at the U.S. Open at Inverness in Toledo, but it wasn't until the Carling Open at Oakland Hills in 1964 that my eyes really opened. He had a shot of about 150 yards to the green, selected an 8-iron and took a little, short swing. I told myself there was no way he was going to get there, but the ball just exploded off the clubface and wound up 10 feet from the pin.

"Where did that come from?" I wondered, and I began to watch more closely some of the peculiarities in Hogan's swing. I noticed that he started his upper body before his lower on the takeaway, which restricted his hips on the backswing. I noticed that the golf club started back parallel to the shoulder line on the takeaway. If his shoulders were parallel to the target line, Hogan's club would swing straight back on the line. But if his shoulders were set open, or left of that target line, the club would swing back *outside* the target line.

And it seemed as if Hogan's swing had two different arcs. It would go out and all of a sudden it would be behind him. It looked as if it had changed directions completely.

More importantly, I noticed that when he was about half-way through his backswing—his hands between the belt and the armpit—his lower body started moving left. It amazed me that his lower body moved forward so early, but I could readily see that Hogan couldn't "hit from the top" with that kind of action. There was no way the right side could be brought into play too early with that swing.

Those observations set me on the right path, but it wasn't easy. The first thing I did was hit thousands of balls trying to start my hips down before I got my club to the top of the backswing. I just couldn't relate to this. It was like trying to throw a baseball while running backward. From there, I went up a lot of bad roads before I made an important discovery.

I had always found success when I relaxed my right side at address and concentrated on starting the club back with my left hand or arm. I was fairly certain that was one of the keystones to successful shotmaking. I was convinced that the downswing was the result of the backswing. I had an intuition that some day I would find a way of starting the club back that would make the downswing happen naturally and correctly.

I had tried taking the club away with my shoulders, but I always turned them late so my pattern would be to start with my arms. Even when I'd think of starting with my shoulders, they would follow the movement of my hands. This usually produced a tilting movement of the shoulders.

One day I was playing in a tournament. I had been hitting the ball to the right and was determined to purposely hook my shots. The first thing I tried was to take the club inside the target line going back. I'd had success with this in the past because it tends to put right-to-left hook spin on the ball. But if you take the club inside too quickly you have to lift it. Otherwise your backswing stays flat somewhere down around your waist. Lifting the club ruins the swing plane or clubhead path that produces the right-to-left action I wanted.

I was desperate, because I couldn't turn the ball to the left, when suddenly something told me—*take your left shoulder to the inside.* I had never tried that. I had been playing golf since I was 10, teaching professionally for six years, and I had tried a million different ways of taking the club back. But never this one.

So I swung my left shoulder to the inside, and immediately felt things happening that had never happened before. I began to realize that I was making more of a horizontal than vertical movement with my shoulders. Instead of tilting them, I was starting a turn with my shoulders. Also they were turning *sooner* than they ever had before. Right away my shots took on a different look, shooting out on a super trajectory that was lower and had good carry and lots of roll.

A couple of days later my father was watching me hit shots, and I asked him if the club was going inside. He said it wasn't. I was turning my left shoulder *inside,* but the club was going *straight back.* This excited me, because I knew that's what I had always wanted. If I took my left shoulder to the inside, the club went back on a line parallel to my shoulders at address. From there I knew it would get behind me. Hogan's kind of clubhead path, in other words.

Another important thing was happening. My father had always told me I had an up-and-down type swing. This didn't give me as much extension through the ball as the player who swings around and onto the line. But now I had that extension, and my father was amazed. He'd never seen me look like that before.

Within just a few days, things began falling into place.
I suffered setbacks, and I tried variations. I realized that my
first inspiration—to take the shoulder inside—needed
refinement. But gradually my swing evolved into one which
was achieving what I felt was the greatest possible windup
on the backswing. This created a tautness in the back
muscles so intense that I felt my lower body moving forward
before I could get the club completely back.

That's the way Hogan always had looked to me. I knew I
had found my swing. Since then, although teaching has been
my main job, I've had much more success as a player,
winning the 1968 New York State PGA Championship,
among other accomplishments.

More important to me is the success I've had with my
method in improving the games of my pupils ranging from
high-handicappers at my club to professionals. Among the
latter who have adopted my method is Gene Borek, now the
head professional at La Gorce Country Club in Miami. Gene
was Player of the Year in the Metropolitan (N.Y.) PGA
Section in 1974 and shot an eye-popping 65 in the second
round of the 1973 U.S. Open at Oakmont.

I won't guarantee that using my method will transform you
into a player of professional tour caliber. I will guarantee that
it will improve your game—and quickly. Because the method
is so simple and clears away much of the confusion
surrounding the golf swing, it will help you to some extent
if you do no more than read this book. After that, it's up to
you. There is no magic to it. The amount you improve
depends on how hard you want to work. But the
boundaries are limitless.

Carl Lohren
Glen Cove, N.Y.
February, 1975

CHAPTER ONE: THE MOVE –WHAT IT IS AND HOW TO MAKE IT

The purpose of a golf swing is to deliver a blow with an implement that will send a small ball flying far and in the desired direction.

Sounds simple enough, doesn't it? It isn't. To strike the ball far and straight, that implement—your golf club—must be swung with enough speed, at the proper angle of descent and on the proper path. Right away you've got yourself all kinds of complications.

There is nothing natural about the golf swing. If somebody says you are a natural golfer, he means you have excellent coordination. That helps, but it still doesn't get you halfway home. Ben Hogan once said that the first time you pick up a golf club, every instinct that comes to your mind is wrong. Watch a child the first time he or she is given a golf club and told to swing at a ball. The club is picked straight up and delivered with a strong right-sided blow as if the ball were a log waiting to be split with an ax.

Overcoming this instinct to hit *at* the ball with the dominant right side has been the curse of the golfer since the game was invented. Proposed solutions have filled countless pages of golf instruction through the years. Countless dollars have been poured into the pockets of countless teaching professionals by pupils searching desperately for the way. By the time the average player has been inundated with all the theories of arm movement, leg movement, weight shift to and fro, wrist cocking and uncocking, hand action and other components of the complex golf swing, his mind is spinning so rapidly he has very little chance of understanding what a good swing is, let alone making one.

Right now I'm going to give you one thought that will clear away the fog, one move that correctly done will give you an effective, repeating golf swing that will send you on your way to a lifetime of better golf.

Start your swing with your left shoulder. At the moment of takeaway, the very beginning of the backswing, start your left shoulder *turning around your spine*. One small area of the body . . . one move. I'm not asking you to change your swing. I just want you to give it *a new start*.

That probably sounds too simple to believe, but the whole secret of this system is here, at the start of your swing. To get the shoulders turning around correctly, you must think of starting the left shoulder *forward* in the direction you're facing, rather than around. This will start the shoulders turning around the spine on the right track (see illustration #1).

Most golf instructors stress that a turn must occur, but they attach no significance to *when* it takes place.

1. MOVE SHOULDER FORWARD TO START THE SWING

The correct starting move of the left shoulder must be forward. The two larger illustrations, viewed from a position that looks directly down at the top of the shoulders, show how this forward move immediately starts the shoulders swinging around the spine, which acts like a fixed axis for your backswing. Note that the hands and arms have not swung back sharply to the inside. This move extends the club back along a path that follows the shoulder line. The smaller drawings (far right) emphasize the starting thought you should have—move your left shoulder forward to start your swing (top). Your thought should be only to start the swing. Once you have started it forward, let the rest of your swing happen naturally.

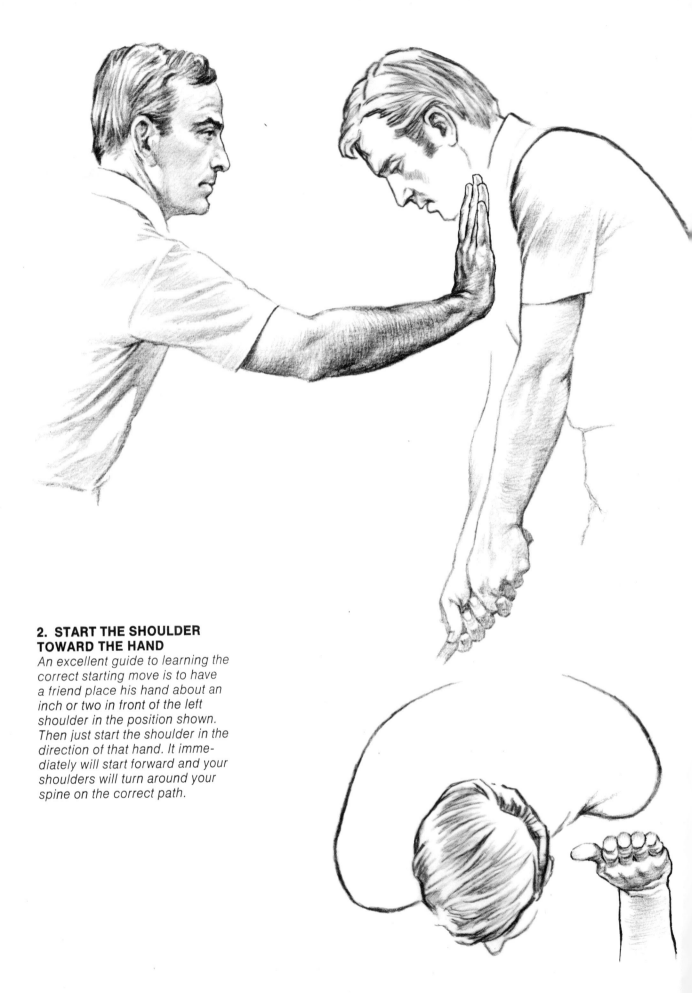

2. START THE SHOULDER TOWARD THE HAND

An excellent guide to learning the correct starting move is to have a friend place his hand about an inch or two in front of the left shoulder in the position shown. Then just start the shoulder in the direction of that hand. It immediately will start forward and your shoulders will turn around your spine on the correct path.

I believe it must be the first thing that happens in your swing. The first and only action you need think about is to start the left shoulder forward. Since this one move is going to make you a better striker of the golf ball, I'm going to dwell on it at some length.

The important thing to understand about this move and the action that follows is that the shoulders turn rather than tilt in relation to the spine. On the backswing, they revolve around your spine much as a searchlight sweeps around a lighthouse, at right angles to your spine.

That proper revolution will be accomplished if you simply think of starting to turn your left shoulder forward in the direction you're facing. I emphasize that I'm only talking about a *start*. The rest of the turn will follow naturally. I don't want you to think about anything except starting this move, for reasons I'll explain later.

To help some of my pupils gain an immediate awareness of the correct starting move I often face them as they address the ball. I hold my hand a few inches in front of the left shoulder, as shown in illustration #2, and simply tell them to start the shoulder toward the palm of my hand.

When I discuss the left shoulder I'm not talking about a spot. I'm talking about the entire left shoulder area, the upper left side of your trunk. I've never seen a player make a good, honest shoulder movement without having the shoulder, upper arm, back and chest area move simultaneously (see illustration #3).

When the left shoulder swings out, the right shoulder of course swings back. This movement, this swinging of the two shoulders around the spine, is what maintains the axis for your swing. It also is a big factor in creating the windup of the back muscles which results in that all-important windup.

Here is a drill that will help you identify the correct starting move. Stand perfectly erect and hold a club in a vertical position with your arms extended straight out in front of you, as shown in illustration #4. Be sure that you remain perfectly relaxed as you do the following. Start the left shoulder forward so that the shoulders turn in a perfect horizontal plane. This drill should help you capture the correct feeling. Remember that the upper body must start turning before the lower. You can gradually lower your arms and the club while practicing this drill until you are able to make the correct starting move from your normal address position. If you have trouble learning to move the upper left side correctly, here are two more key thoughts that may help you to make this move:

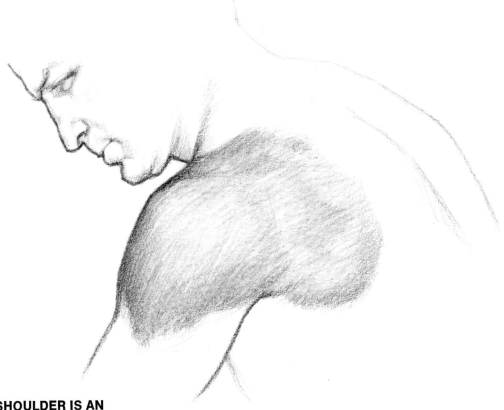

3. THE SHOULDER IS AN AREA, NOT A SPOT

When starting the swing with your left shoulder, your thought should not be concentrated on one spot but rather on the entire area of the shoulder and upper left side illustrated here.

4. PRACTICE THE MOVE FROM ERECT STANCE

This drill may help you start correctly when you first try to make the move. Stand in a perfectly erect position (right), arms extended straight out, holding a club in a vertical position while remaining relaxed. Then make the move in a perfectly horizontal plane, simply by starting the left shoulder forward. Remember that the upper body must start turning before the lower. This feeling can quickly be adapted to a normal address position.

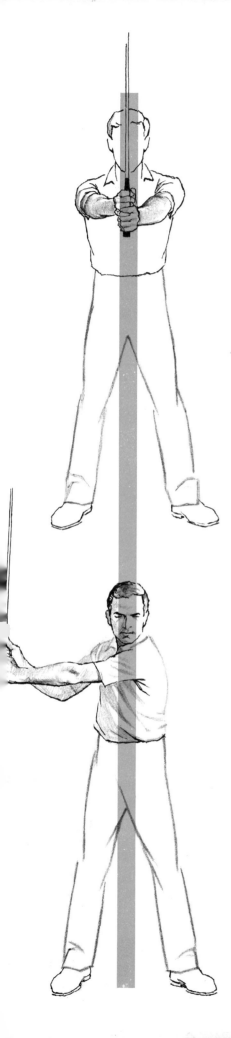

1. Think of starting to make a small U-turn with that left shoulder. Again, concern yourself only with the start and not with trying to turn the shoulder all the way. Imagine starting the left shoulder turning to where the right shoulder is. It won't get there, but it has been a helpful concept to many of my pupils (see illustration #5).

2. Visualize your upper body being in a tube; turn your left shoulder—and with it your right—in a perfect arc within that tube, without moving your body even one degree laterally. It may help you to feel as if you are turning in a *small* area rather than a larger one to start winding the muscles as soon as possible (see illustration #5).

Make this move in a relaxed manner, with a complete absence of tension in the upper body. Any tenseness when you get ready to start the swing will result in an inability to make this move properly. But if you are properly relaxed, this initial move is your transport to success. This one simple act creates a correct golf swing, encouraging a natural, almost instinctive return into the forward swing.

One of the major problems in the golf swing is that battle to keep the left side in control while the right tries to overpower it at the wrong time. Please understand that the right side certainly is vital in the golf swing. It helps provide the power that gives you distance in your shots. So the right side must come into play, but only at the proper time, with the left side still in control as it guides the swing through the area of impact with the ball and gives you the accuracy which golf demands.

Unfortunately, this proper application of right-side power goes against our basic instincts. When our arms and hands get as far back as they can go and we subconsciously face the prospect of hitting that ball sitting motionless down there, our stronger right side is commanded to spring into action.

That's our ruination. Almost every missed shot is the result of the right side overpowering the left at the beginning of the downswing or any time prior to impact. When you top the ball, when you hit a "fat" shot in which you strike the ground before the ball, when you pull or hook the ball to the left, or slice a shot from left to right—the overly active right side is the culprit in almost every case.

But when the left side does not yield control, when you are able to return clubface to ball with the left in command until it is time for the right to act, when you have found a way to subdue those right side instincts at that critical moment when the backswing changes into the forward swing, you can produce a swing that delivers more powerful, accurate shots than you ever thought possible.

The one move I've given you accomplishes this. But before you accept it, you naturally want to know why it happens and why you should trust it to happen as I say it does. Read on.

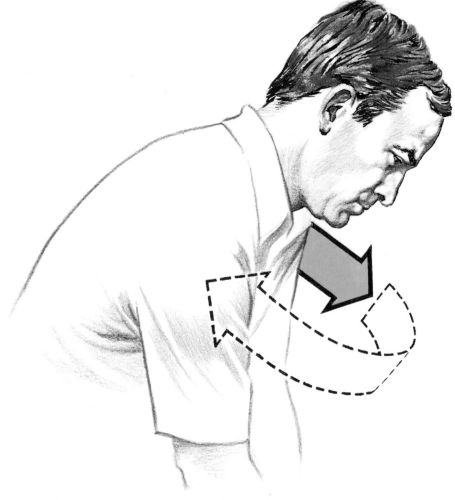

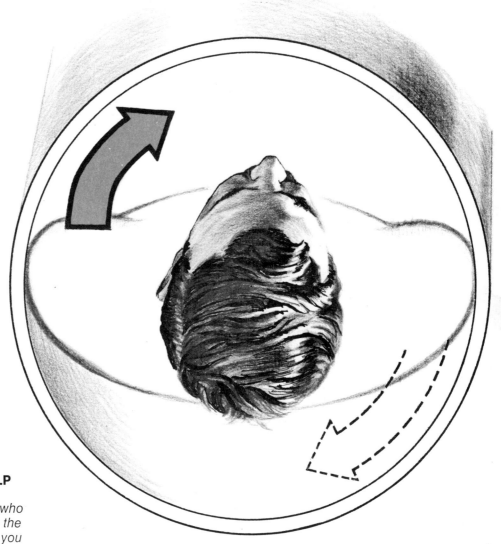

5. TWO THOUGHTS TO HELP YOU MOVE UPPER BODY

Here are two drills for people who have trouble learning to move the upper left side. They will help you get oriented to moving the left shoulder correctly. Think of starting to make a small U-turn with the left shoulder (left). Imagine it turning to where the right shoulder is. But only think of starting it there, not trying to turn it all the way. You can also visualize your upper body being in a tube (right). Turn your left shoulder, and of course your right, in a perfect arc within that tube, without moving laterally at all. These two drills will not, in and of themselves, result in the sound swing that the move creates. They are only aids for people who find it difficult to get the upper left side moving.

CHAPTER TWO: WHY THE MOVE WORKS

Most golfers pull the swing apart and try to learn it bit by bit. The significance of this method is that it puts everything together. I submit that starting your swing with the left shoulder causes all the right things to happen without your having to think about them. In this chapter, I will explain the reasons that it does.

As you progress with this method, you naturally will encounter roadblocks and will wander away from the basic concept, perhaps without your own awareness. When this happens, return to this chapter and review the fundamentals I'm about to describe. They will re-implant in your mind what this one move does to establish the total concept of the golf swing, renewing the guidelines against which you should test every quirk or gimmick you might want to try in your swing.

The one move I described in Chapter 1—starting the left shoulder forward first—establishes four fundamentals which have been incorporated into virtually every great golf swing in history. These four fundamentals are interrelated; one does not function as effectively without the others. Together they give you the correct golf swing we're after. One of the features of this swing is that the forward swing will react to the backswing, almost like a reflex.

You do not have to worry about accomplishing the four fundamentals. As I said, the one move does that for you. But so you will be aware of what is happening and can have some guideposts for your swing in the future, let's examine them separately.

FUNDAMENTAL I

The first of these fundamentals is to *maintain your vertical axis on your backswing.* This axis is, in effect, your spine. Liken this axis to that lighthouse around which the search-light revolves, or to the axis around which a schoolroom globe turns. The spine, your axis, must remain fixed as your shoulders turn around it on the backswing.

Maintaining this backswing axis does two things:

- It helps build up and retain power by keeping you from swaying during the backswing.

- By keeping your swing in one place, it helps you return the clubface at impact square to or facing the target, in the same position it was at address.

Starting your swing with the left shoulder immediately insures maintenance of your axis.

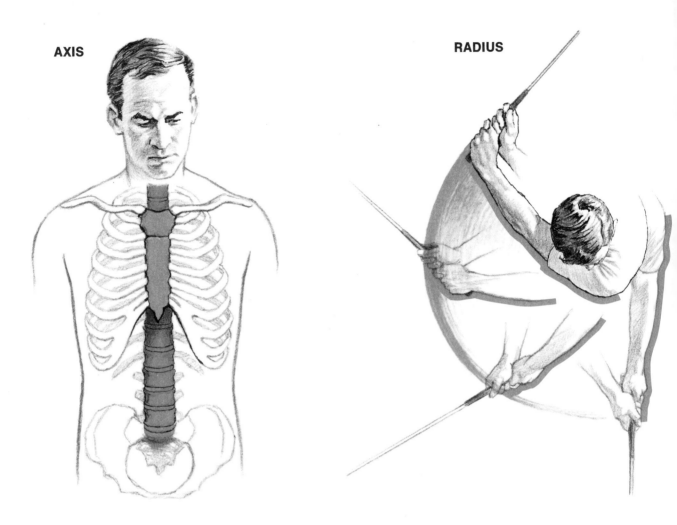

AXIS

RADIUS

FUNDAMENTAL II

The second fundamental is to *keep the radius of your left arm swing the same* from the beginning of the swing through impact. This radius is the span from the left shoulder to the left hand. Maintaining it does three things:

- It returns the clubhead to the spot behind the ball from which it started, neither higher nor lower.

- It insures maximum width of the arc of your swing.

- It contributes to the buildup of clubhead speed and power.

Starting the swing with a correct, early move of the left shoulder eliminates unwanted influence from the hands and allows the left arm to swing freely with full radius.

FUNDAMENTAL III

The third fundamental is to keep your swing *within the boundaries of your swing plane*. The swing plane is the line your club follows as you swing up and down. You establish this plane at address. It can be pictured as an imaginary line drawn from the toe of the club up over your shoulders. Envision this plane as a flat surface—a pane of glass, for example—leaning against that line and placed along the

6. THE FOUR FUNDAMENTALS IN AN EFFECTIVE SWING

Establishment and maintenance of the four fundamentals illustrated here result in the factors which produce an effective golf swing. Starting the left shoulder early allows you to maintain your vertical axis on the backswing. It maintains the radius or width of your swing arc. It keeps your swing on its correct plane, which guides you in making the swing in the proper direction. In combination, these fundamentals contribute to the windup of your upper body muscles which creates speed and power on the forward swing.

PLANE

WINDUP

line of your shoulders. Your swing can fall below that line but should never rise above it and break the imaginary pane of glass anytime during the backswing.

If it did break the glass, your forward swing would approach the ball from too steep an angle and drive your club into the ground, not the ball.

Moving the left shoulder first starts the swing in the correct plane. It prevents the body or arms from throwing your swing outside that plane. Maintaining this correct backswing plane keeps your swing in the right direction, insuring that on the forward swing the clubhead will approach the ball from a direction inside the target line, giving you maximum leverage and power on the forward swing.

You should not try to consciously follow your plane. Making the one move with the left shoulder does it for you and keeps the club swinging on the proper path.

FUNDAMENTAL IV

The fourth fundamental is to *begin winding your upper body early so that it can wind up fully*. This induces as a reflex the correct forward swing and contributes most of the power in your swing. An early windup does three things:

- It ensures that you will stretch the muscles in the upper left side of your body.

7. RESULTS CREATED BY THE FOUR FUNDAMENTALS

When the four fundamentals described on the previous two pages are established in your swing early, you encourage three desirable results in your forward swing. A) The left side is in a position of control because the arms and hands have not outraced your swing to the top. B) Your left leg moves early and leads the downswing, providing a proper platform for your forward swing. C) The correct windup keeps the right arm and shoulder (shaded area) from acting too early in the downswing. In the position shown here, the right side muscles are just beginning to release their full power as a reaction to a correct unwinding of the body and the centrifugal force of the swing. If you have started your swing correctly, all of these results will happen almost as a reflex without conscious thought or trying on your part.

A

● It removes the slack from your swing, creating a force against the lower body so intense that your instinct is to relieve that force by moving into the forward swing with your left side leading, not the right.

● It keeps the right side from taking over when it might otherwise want to at the beginning of that forward swing.

The creation of windup and the subsequent reaction to it is vital in producing a sound swing. But this windup can be effective only if it is accompanied by the other three fundamentals—maintaining your axis on the backswing, keeping your swing radius the same from start to impact and swinging your club on the proper plane. Without these fundamentals, the benefits of a good windup would be dissipated.

So the one move of your left shoulder, the start of a simple turn around your axis or spine, establishes these four fundamentals immediately into your swing. It maintains your vertical axis on the backswing; it keeps the radius of your left arm the same from beginning of swing to impact; it keeps your swing within the boundaries of your swing plane; it winds the upper body early so that it can wind up

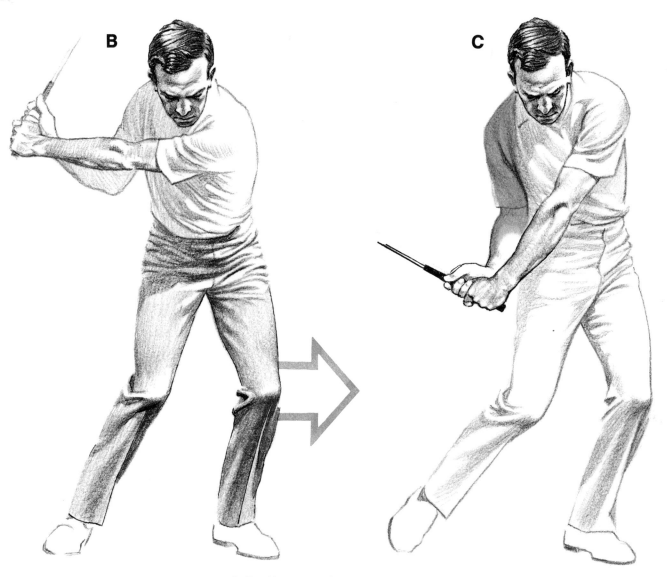

fully. If you make the move correctly, you don't need to think about doing anything else. Your forward swing will be a result of starting correctly, a reaction that gives you the factors that make for longer, straighter shots.

You gain left-side control because the instinct of the right side to hit is subordinated at the moment the hands and arms get as far back as they can go in the backswing. As I said a moment ago, this is because the windup in the left side has created a force so great that the instinct to relieve it is much greater than the anxiety to hit with the right side.

The confrontation between the left and the right is further staved off because the starting movement of your left shoulder induces a clubhead path which delays the arrival of the arms and hands at the top of the swing. In effect, this means that your shoulders and upper back will coil fully and be ready to start the return swing before your arms and hands have reached a position where they might take control.

Because you start your shoulder forward and because you create the great windup in the muscles of your upper left side, the left leg—which is closer to the target—moves early and leads on the forward swing. This provides the platform

for the successful completion of your swing through
the shot.

The most important result is that all the power you create
in your swing is allowed to explode at the proper moment.
This is nothing you consciously do. It is something that just
happens. You will get the feeling that your lower body is
pulling your arms through the swing, your left side in control.
This keeps the right side—the shoulder, arm and hip—from
acting until the simple buildup of clubhead speed through
centrifugal force allows them to release at the proper
moment just before impact with the ball, hence the
explosion of power.

So much for power. How about accuracy? To hit golf shots
straight, the club obviously must be swung in the intended
direction. In my opinion, golfers *instinctively* will hit the ball
where they are aiming, provided nothing interferes with this
natural instinct.

The right side wants to interfere, especially as the club is
swung faster. The key to straightness, then, is insuring that
the right side will not intervene too early and force the swing
in the wrong direction.

We have learned that starting the swing with the left
shoulder subdues the right side by establishing the fundamentals involving axis, radius, plane and windup, resulting in
a release of right-side power that does not come too early.
This allows the instincts to direct your swing toward the
intended target. It helps explain why good players can use
their instincts more effectively than poor players.

(A word here for left-handers—simply transpose the words
"left" and "right" wherever they appear. This method is
equally effective for you.)

I said that starting the left shoulder turning around the
spine helps create windup. But it won't create maximum
windup unless the upper body starts turning *before* the lower.
This encourages a *separation* between the upper and lower
body that allows the upper body to turn more than the
lower. That's what creates the maximum power windup. This
happens because you have made an early shoulder turn
. . . and by *early* I mean *first.* If your lower body turns at the
same time as your shoulders, you lose a lot of the
muscle windup.

I caution you that your upper body needs to beat the lower
at the start by just a fraction of a second. *I do not want you to
hold back the hips and legs.* If you think about holding back
your hips, it can distract you from starting your left shoulder
first. Then the arms and hands instinctively will take over. If

8. HOW TO DEVELOP FEEL OF SEPARATION

To learn the feeling of separation between your upper and lower body, sit in a straight (not swivel) chair, trunk erect, arms extended in a relaxed manner closely approximating the address position (illustration at right). Then rotate your shoulders until you feel tension in the back (below). Because your hips are fixed in the sitting position, you'll quickly identify the sensation of your upper body turning before the lower. This is what you ideally must incorporate into the start of your normal swing.

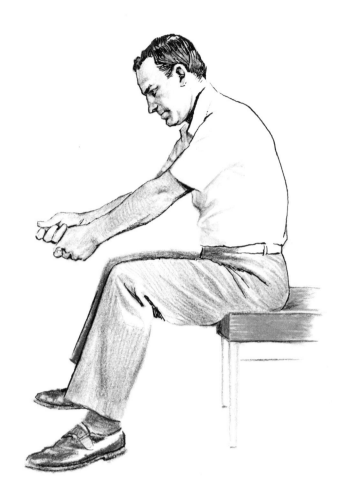

you restrict your lower body too long your shoulders won't be able to continue on around.

That's why I tell you so positively to think only of *starting* your left shoulder first.

Here is a good exercise to learn the "feel" of separation. Practice hitting short shots, short enough that you need only turn your shoulders without moving your lower body on the backswing. This drill will give you the sensation of separation, of turning your upper body before the lower. Practice should help you incorporate this feeling into your full swing. Another drill that will help you develop the feel of separation is explained in illustration #8.

We read and hear a lot about the "one-piece takeaway." In my opinion, that creates an unwanted picture of the shoulder, arms, hands, club and upper body all moving as a unit in the beginning. This is what happens, but whenever the arms and hands are involved in your mental concept, they'll steal the show. The hands, especially, will jump the gun because they're made up of smaller muscles which always react more quickly. If the hands and arms move first, they won't direct the club in the proper direction. Or you'll think about them too long and create a stiffness in your swing.

So as you start the left shoulder forward, exert no influence on the club with the hands and arms. Don't try to keep them from moving, and don't try to make them move. Don't be afraid that they won't get where they're supposed to go. Even though you're relaxed and gripping the club lightly—a point I'll discuss at some length later—your arms and hands will go at the same time as your shoulders. They're connected.

Let me give you here two important points that are inextricably bound together: you should think only of *starting* the left shoulder for the last split-second of time spent standing over the ball; and you should allow yourself to swing back at your natural speed and tempo.

I don't agree with the opinion that the club should be taken away slowly on the backswing. I'll grant you that an artificially slow tempo helps a player who is guilty of bad mechanics on the takeaway, whose hands and arms get ahead of his shoulders, who loses the backswing axis or tilts his shoulders instead of turning them. If he swings back slowly he gives his shoulders a chance to instinctively catch up; he has more time to recover and make a better forward swing through the ball.

But if you establish the correct backswing axis, radius and swing plane and begin to build windup with your initial move, you can have the luxury of starting your swing with whatever

9. CLOSE YOUR EYES TO FEEL THE MOVE

Many players are ball-bound, wanting to strike at the ball instead of swinging through it. This can inhibit you in making the correct starting move. This drill can help you build an awareness of the move as you begin hitting shots. Simply address the ball, then shut your eyes and make your swing. Be sure there is no one in the immediate vicinity the first few times, but soon you will be able to start your swing correctly and swing without worrying about the ball.

10. DRILL WITH RIGHT FINGERS OFF THE SHAFT

If you have a particularly dominant right side, it may be difficult for you, at first, to allow the correct starting move to work. Here is a drill that will help. Hold the club in your usual grip. Then open the fingers of the right hand leaving the hand itself in position on the club. This will remove any right side influence and allow the correct starting move to direct the left arm and club back on the proper path. A further, and more difficult, step is to remove the right hand from the club completely and swing with the left alone. You can add more right-hand grip gradually as you build the correct feel of the start of the swing.

natural tempo is compatible with your instincts.

A warning here—you may feel that your swing is faster than it has been. Just remember that you are starting your swing in your natural tempo now. It may be true that your hands and clubhead are traveling faster than you are used to. This is the result of building swing power from the center. It's the old crack-the-whip analogy. The outer end always moves faster than the inner, more fixed portion.

The result will be a gradual acceleration of your swing speed. This will create the greatest possible extension of the radius—imagine a weight being slung and extended on the end of a rope. The gradual acceleration will cause a natural hinging of the wrists. The arms and club will move backward after the back muscles are fully wound, putting you in the best situation for an instinctive return of the forward swing through the ball.

A long thought, *the thought of swinging the shoulder around instead of just starting it,* can be detrimental to your swing. If you try to mentally guide the shoulder around instead of just letting it happen you can retard the natural acceleration of your swing. *Starting* the shoulder correctly, that is, forward, insures completion of the shoulder turn, much as a barrel gains speed when you push it off the crest of a hill. I've seen many players with good swings jump at the ball from the top of the backswing because they start too slowly. It registers on their subconscious as incompatible with the speed they instinctively know they're going to need going forward.

With the proper start, the swing will find its own tempo. Simply break inertia with the left shoulder, dismiss any thought of tempo and speed and let your instincts and natural rhythm take over. *Do it with abandon.*

Arnold Palmer is an excellent model for this action. He's been accused of looking like a driving-range drunk when he swings, but he's really just starting those shoulders with carefree abandon, letting his instincts determine the speed and tempo of his swing.

You'll have problems doing this for awhile, because you won't be used to having things so simple. Right now you probably don't accept the fact that you can make a whole golf swing—and a good one—with just one little move. But I urge you not to add things to this swing, to complicate it.

Again, I stress that the swing is a whole. One objective of this book is to give you a method that will allow you to perform the swing as a whole instead of one that requires various manipulations.

11. PITFALLS TO AVOID WHEN STARTING THE SWING

Here are three common pitfalls to guard against in learning the correct starting move. A) The arms are tense, with the right arm too straight instead of slightly bent and relaxed. This tenseness locks the muscles of your neck and shoulders preventing you from making a free move and starting the left shoulder correctly. B) The club is being swung inside the flight path too quickly by the hands and arms. Any independent movement of the hands and arms will cancel the influence of the shoulder move, and thus reduce your chances of establishing the correct fundamentals at the very beginning of your swing. C) The upper and lower body are starting back together. There must be a separation of the two that allows the upper body to turn more than the lower. That's what creates maximum windup and power. The cylinders (below right) illustrate proper separation at takeaway. The upper and lower are together at address, but the upper body turns before the lower when the backswing is begun.

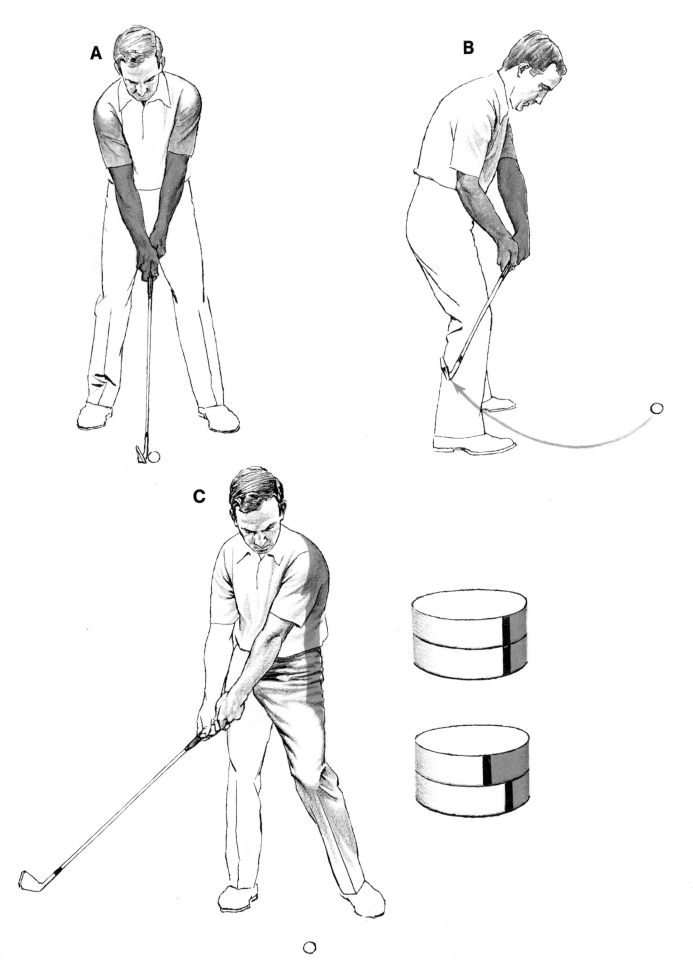

CHAPTER THREE: HOW THE MOVE ACCOMPLISHES GOLF'S FUNDAMENTALS

You now know what fundamentals are established by the initial move and what they accomplish. This is all you will need to make the move properly and to improve your golf shots. However, some readers may want a more detailed explanation of how and why these principles work. This chapter is for them. Beginning golfers would be best advised to skip this chapter, and return to it only when they have thoroughly mastered the move and the preparation procedures in Chapter 4.

Let's now review the four swing fundamentals and their functions, but this time in greater technical detail. Again, this section is largely for the more advanced golfing student.

MAINTAINING VERTICAL AXIS

The key to any repeating golf swing is the maintenance of a vertical backswing axis. Without it you cannot build maximum windup and are not likely to achieve a consistent plane.

The vertical axis, in effect, is your spine. Maintaining that axis on the backswing is important for at least three reasons. It provides a center around which to turn the shoulders and fully wind the back muscles to create windup. It provides a fixed point around which you swing your arms and club to keep the backswing plane constant. And it's vital in getting you into a position from which you can strike the ball most effectively. If you move this axis on your backswing, it's harder to relate to what you're trying to hit (see illustration #12).

So it's very important that this axis doesn't move forward, backward, up, down or sideways. Unfortunately, there are many ways of taking the club away which promote just such movements. If you take the club away with your hands and arms, your left shoulder could tilt excessively and pull the axis to the right. If you pick the club up too quickly because you are thinking of swinging it away with your hands and arms instead of starting the left shoulder, you could sway forward, especially if the left shoulder drops or tilts. Similarly, if you are thinking too intently of taking the club back inside the target line with your hands and arms, you could be pulled backward. Thinking of making a wide arc could pull you off your axis.

There are two common causes of swaying to the left on the backswing. One is letting the hips start turning simultaneously with the shoulders, sometimes causing a shoulder sway to the left or reverse pivot. The other is actually starting the swing with a lateral movement of the hips to the right which causes the shoulders to tip laterally to the left.

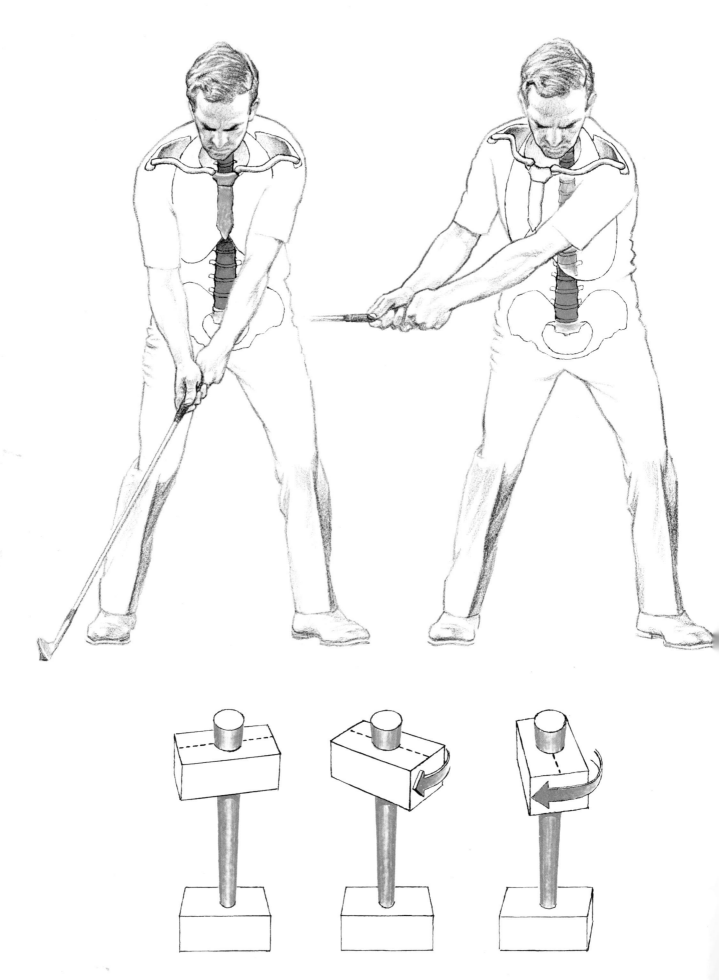

12. STEADY AXIS ON BACKSWING GIVES SWING A FIXED CENTER

Your vertical axis is, in effect, your spine. It is important to keep this axis steady on the backswing so that your swing will have a fixed center. The cutaway views (above) show how the axis is maintained by starting the left shoulder turning around it. This contributes greatly to the buildup of power and keeps the upper body in place during the backswing. The model below shows graphically how the axis remains in position as the shoulders rotate around it at right angles.

The vertical axis can also be referred to as the vertical line of balance. Now, you could have a good player who gets away with poor mechanics because he's a fine athlete with a good sense of balance. But if you're like most of us and don't concentrate on achieving sound mechanical technique, you're much more likely to fall into one of the above ways of losing your axis, simply because your instincts aren't good enough for you to counteract the bad moves and maintain your balance.

Good mechanics? Just that left shoulder again. Start it around. At the same time your right shoulder moves back. Your shoulders now are rotating at right angles around your spine, and that effectively fixes your axis. Simple, isn't it?

This move eliminates the need to concern yourself with various manipulations. For example, you don't have to worry about keeping your weight from going to the outside of your right foot or keeping your head still, a couple of bromides that even the rankest beginner has heard repeatedly. Your weight will not go to the outside of your right foot because your body will turn *around* the axis rather than sway laterally. The fact that your arms are swung to the right around the axis will properly take pressure to the right leg, but it will never go beyond where it's supposed to be. In my view, there is no point in trying to keep the weight on the inside of the right foot as is commonly advised, because that might inhibit the natural movement created by starting the left shoulder out. You don't want to set up any roadblocks.

A steady head is a *result*, not a *cause*. Trying to keep the head still while turning your body freely at the beginning of the swing is like pickles and milk—it's a conflict of interests. It can make you too ballbound, too stationary, interfering with a free body turn and the extension of the radius. If you concentrate on keeping your head still rather than starting your left shoulder out, everything else suffers.

MAINTAINING THE RADIUS

As I noted earlier, the radius of the arm swing is the distance from the left shoulder to the left hand. When the arms and hands are directed on the backswing by the upper left side or shoulder, the club will take the longest route allowed by the length of your arms. This gives your upper body a better chance to get fully coiled before the hands reach the end of the backswing. This means there will be an uncoiling of the body before the hands can make a move on the forward swing (see illustration #13).

In establishing a good radius, we want to be sure to main-

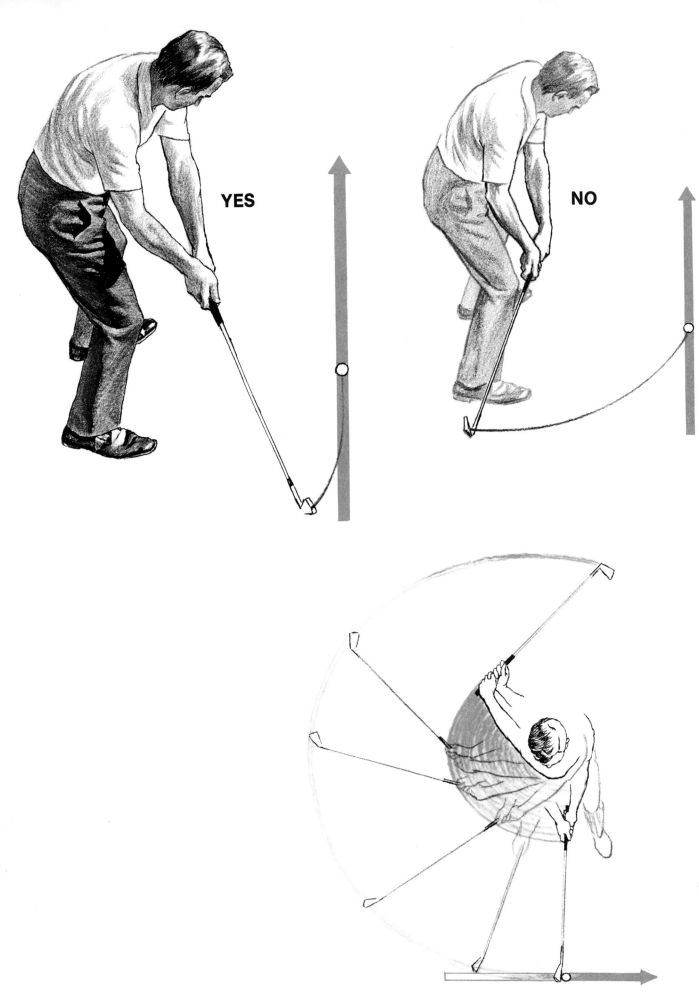

YES

NO

44

tain a steady backswing axis. Here is where many golfers run into trouble. If you consciously try to produce a big swing arc by trying to stretch your arms to the rear, you tend to pull the shoulder *down* in a tilting fashion and move the axis in the same direction your arms are going. Now you are accomplishing a wide arc and lots of extension, but you are not coiling your back muscles at the begining of the swing, so your hands get to the top too soon.

Taking the club back low can help you create a good radius but it can also distort the backswing axis. Starting the club back inside the target line doesn't direct the radius on the longest route.

I'm not saying the club cannot be swung back with the arms and hands. Many good players do. But they all turn their shoulders *more* than their lower body, so they get some windup. Often they don't get enough early windup to keep the right side from creeping into the act before it should. We're looking for a better way.

As far as I'm concerned, starting the left shoulder forward is the best way of directing your club on the longest route and maintaining your axis at the same time. Your arms can be relaxed because you are not making a conscious effort to move them. In that state they can be directed—you might even think of them as being slung—back on a line parallel to the shoulder line at address by the initial movement of the left shoulder.

Maximum extension of the radius is most easily accomplished by centrifugal force. Assuming you are relaxed at address, the correct turning action started by your left shoulder induces a gradual acceleration that will extend the radius naturally and effortlessly. The chest does not create a roadblock because it turns out of the way. The left arm is being extended as far away from the body as it can be. In other words, your club is taking the longest possible route to the top of the backswing.

When the left shoulder has turned about to your chin the clubhead will have swung about as far as it can go if you have maintained your backswing axis. At this point, something almost magical happens. In observing the swings of players who make this move well, the club seems suddenly to get behind them in perfect position from which to return on the downswing. It appears to change directions almost abruptly. It doesn't, of course. What happens is that the club is being swung in the natural arc established by the turning of the shoulders rather than being picked up by an independent action of the arms and hands.

13. MAINTAIN FULL RADIUS FOR WIDE SWING ARC

The radius of the arm swing is the distance from the left shoulder to the left hand. When the arm and hand are directed on the backswing by the left shoulder it encourages this radius to swing back at maximum width and along the proper path (top left). This ensures that the club will take the longest route allowed by the length of your arms. This is desirable because you want the clubhead to return to the same spot behind the ball from which it started. An improper or diminished radius results (above right) when the left arm and clubhead are pulled too quickly inside that target line. The bottom view shows the radius of the left arm and also the clubhead, the latter being modified only by the cocking of the wrists. When this radius is maintained, it encourages a completion of the backswing turn before the hands can reach the top and interfere with a correct downswing reaction.

14. PLANE KEEPS BACKSWING ON RIGHT TRACK

The swing plane is the angle at which the club is swung up and down, relative to the ground. A plane is actually a flat surface. The swing plane thus can be visualized as a pane of glass that leans against an imaginary line drawn from the toe of the club at address up over the shoulders and placed along the line of the shoulders. This plane marks the ideal track the clubhead should follow on the backswing. This is correctly activated by the start of the left shoulder. You should not break that pane of glass on your back-swing. The illustrations below show two theoretical planes established at address. The upright plane at left is normal for taller players or those with short arms; the flatter plane at right is normal for shorter players, or those with long arms.

Hogan's swing was a perfect example of this. He actually swung the club back rather fast. But it looked as if it took him forever to complete his backswing because the clubhead was taking such a long route to the top. Suddenly he was there, already delivering the forward blow because he had made no manipulations to distort his swing radius and thus that natural arc he had created.

One final thought on radius—if you fail to establish a full radius with the left arm, the right side has a chance to take over. The radius has the best chance of being maintained when it is directed the long route by the left shoulder. This delays the arrival of the hands to the top of your swing which allows your shoulders to finish turning and the forward swing reaction to take place before the right side can intervene. And that's really what we're trying to achieve with this method.

ESTABLISHING A PLANE

The theoretical plane at address is the flat surface I described in Chapter 2. The surface, or pane of glass, leans against your shoulders at an angle formed by that imaginary line drawn from the toe of your clubhead up over your shoulders. What this theoretical plane does is give you a guide for the backswing. The clubhead should not be allowed to break this imaginary pane of glass on the backswing (see illustration #14).

I don't advocate either a flat or an upright plane. You establish your backswing plane by your posture at address. That will vary as a player's physical characteristics vary.

In the actual swing, there are two planes—one for the backswing, another, flatter one for the forward swing. How much the two planes vary depends again on your physical characteristics and on how early the lower left side moves forward on the downswing. I'll explain that in a moment.

Starting your left shoulder first gives you the essential ingredient necessary for creating and maintaining a constant backswing plane. The path the arms and hands take becomes compatible with the path of the shoulders.

I hasten to point out here that the path the clubhead follows on the takeaway is directly related to the alignment of the shoulders at address, a subject I'll cover thoroughly in Chapter 4. If the shoulders are aligned parallel with the target line, the clubhead will be extended back straight along the target line. If the shoulders are open at address, as I prefer, the clubhead actually will be started back *outside* the target line. This is a phenomenon very apparent in the swing of Lee Trevino.

Starting your left shoulder first insures that you will swing the left arm and hand down the line without distorting the plane. When you get nervous and tight, as we all do at certain times during a round of golf, the arms and hands might take the golf club away in any direction. It's much more dependable to simply start the left shoulder around in the right direction.

In the ideal golf swing, the forward swing plane is lower than the backswing plane. This happens because the first move on the downswing is a lateral movement of the left leg toward the target. Because the shoulders are turned, this movement causes the right side to be dropped into a lower and more submissive position. It also puts the club in position to return through the ball from a direction more inside the target line. This makes it easier to begin the forward swing with the necessary left-side control and insures that you won't wheel around and "come over the top."

Don't be afraid that this move will give you a flatter back-swing. If you happen to have had an upright swing, you may end up in a less vertical position at the top than you're used to, but there are advantages to this. And if you have been a very flat swinger, the move probably will make your swing more upright. You undoubtedly have been swinging the club inside and around your body with your arms and hands instead of letting the left shoulder propel them straight back and up along the correct path.

The most important advantage of the less vertical plane is that it gets the club behind you. This is essential, because it makes it easier for the forward swing to follow the correct path.

In a moment I'll explain lower body movement and how it happens. Right now I want you to be aware of what makes it work most effectively by pointing out what can go wrong if you start your swing with something other than the left shoulder. The club can move above your natural plane at the top of the backswing if it is swung back on too upright an arc. Or it can be swung back so that it points "across the line"—to the right of the target line at the top of the swing. This usually is caused when the arms and hands take the club back inside the target line and then lift it abruptly to complete the backswing. The club can also reach either of these positions at the top if you start the upper and lower body together. To swing the club correctly from either of these positions you would need to make a big adjustment or compensation. There would have to be a strong, conscious lateral leg drive or a manipulation of the arms and hands—or both—to drop the club into a lower plane from which the inside-to-down-the-line blow can be delivered.

Incidentally, this kind of adjusting or compensating can be done, and I'd be the last one to tell you otherwise. The good player who gets himself into an undesirable position at the top will instinctively realize that the only way he can get the club into good striking position is by working his right side inside and "under." But when he does this, he distorts his plane. This costs him some of the power built up through natural acceleration. He would also be more apt to hit the ball off line. He sometimes can salvage the shot, but certainly with no consistency.

The less accomplished player whose club swings back above the plane cannot wind up as fully as he can if he swings back within this plane. Furthermore, he puts his right side in a position to assume command too early. Even if he compensates with a right side action, usually he will get himself blocked out by his right hip. This forces his arm swing out of the proper path and he is then committed to swing "over the top." With his right arm and side now in control, casting the club from outside the target line is inevitable. The buildup of centrifugal force and power is dissipated. The result is a weak pull-slice that goes from left to right, a push-slice that goes from right of the target to farther right, or a pull-hook that goes from left to farther left, depending on what instinctive manipulations he makes with his hands.

Distorting the plane as badly as he has normally would cause his radius to change, too. He often ends up hitting the ball "fat"—striking the ground some distance behind the ball —or topping it.

On the other hand, if you allow the initial movement of the left shoulder to start your swing, it will direct the club on or slightly below the plane in perfect striking position to begin the forward swing. Any need for compensation with the body or manipulation with the arms or hands is eliminated. All you have to do is let the swing happen.

It is my opinion, bolstered by watching many good players, that the best-struck iron shot is one which takes only a thin divot. Show me a player who gouges huge chunks out of the turf and I'll show you one who has started his downswing, more often than not, from a point above his plane. To me, this means only that the club has made too steep a descent into and through the ball. The player who nips the ball, taking a long, thin divot, is returning the club on the widest

possible swing arc. He is able to swing on that wide arc because he has kept his swing in plane. In other words, he can maintain a full swing radius from start to impact because he has not moved the club outside his plane and forced the radius to collapse.

CREATING WINDUP

The last fundamental is windup which, as I said before, is a culmination of all the things that have happened in your swing to this point. In the final analysis, if all else is accomplished, windup is what causes the forward swing to happen correctly.

Let me add another word. *Recoil.* Windup and recoil. Action and reaction to give you an instinctive, consistent and effective swing. For the purists, recoil does not actually happen in a strict physiological sense. But it does happen as a reaction to other factors you have built into the swing. As you will find, it is a very real and very pleasant sensation.

Maximum windup comes from two things—the upper body turning around an axis and the upper body starting before the lower body so that it can turn more than the lower. If all this takes place, the gun is fully loaded to deliver a powerful, on-line blow through the ball.

Of these ingredients, the most important is separation, the starting of the upper body before the lower. It gives you most of your windup and power. That's why in Chapter 2 I made such a point of the necessity of starting the upper left side first. That's why in the next chapter I'm going to set you in an address position that will help you do this when the shoulder starts its move.

When the shoulders have turned as far as they can before the hips move—remember, you're not making any conscious effort to restrict lower body movement—they begin to pull the hips and legs around naturally. This establishes the proper relationship between upper and lower body and allows you to wind the back muscles fully.

Moving the left shoulder first begins your windup immediately. In my view, it enables you to get fully wound before your hands get to the top. Even a little arm or leg movement early can cost you power. Also, it tends to make the club move inside, distorting your plane and shortening your swing path. This invites a contest between the left and the right side at the top of the backswing.

What happens when you reach a state of maximum windup? Your back muscles are wound to a point of such intensity that you can't hold them. This causes the forward

15. START WINDUP EARLY TO GET FULL POWER

Starting the upper left side turning before the lower body and around the axis creates a correct windup of the muscles in the upper back which is the primary source of power in your swing. When they reach a state of maximum windup, these muscles respond almost reflexively on the forward swing in a way that, although technically and anatomically different, behaves very much like the rubber band-driven propeller shown above. This induces a forward swing reaction—not action—that moves your body and the club through in the proper sequence and with a free release of power.

swing reaction. You have created a force, a pressure, so intense that the instinct to alleviate it is greater than your normal anxiety to hit with the right side. This is the way the right side is kept under control at the critical point of exchange between the backswing and the downswing (see illustration #15). In a moment, I'll explain in detail this forward swing reaction.

First, lest you embark on a search for this magical feeling at the top of your backswing, let me point out that *you don't feel the windup on a full shot because it happens so quickly.* A good turn feels like no turn. It will happen almost without your trying to make it happen. After a while, you'll be able to tell whether you've loaded the gun fully by the way the shot goes. Don't look for any unusual feeling at the top of your swing and don't try to achieve it by stretching or otherwise distorting your natural turn.

There is one physical aspect that will be apparent as you learn to build maximum windup—your backswing will shorten. This won't happen immediately, but as you become proficient at making the move you will feel yourself tugged in a forward direction before you finish winding on the backswing. You may feel as if you can't finish your backswing because your left side is moving forward. It's a pleasant feeling, a feeling of having no right-side influence in your swing.

A caution here—don't consciously try to move your left side forward before you finish winding up. These are *results* of proper windup. Any tendency on your part to consciously accomplish them will be detrimental.

What checkpoint should you have on how far back you turn? This depends on your suppleness, length of arms and other physical characteristics. In general, I'd say that if the shoulders rotate more than 90 degrees—so far that the back is facing to the right of the target—there has been a loss of windup right from the beginning. You can tell if you are turning too far if you feel your head, and with it your axis, being pulled to the right as you reach the top of your swing. I can't imagine anybody except an incredibly supple person being able to wind up early, maintain the axis, start the upper body before the lower, maintain the radius well and then rotate more than 90 degrees without destroying that axis.

Theoretically, if you don't destroy your axis you can take your arms and the club as far around as you want. But it's impossible for the average person to get much farther than I've indicated if he's really wound well in the beginning. That's why I'm very suspicious of anybody with a big swing, whose club drops below parallel at the top of the swing. Usually the player has failed to begin winding early, and by overturning he loses much of what he has built up.

I want to emphasize again that if you start properly and begin winding immediately, you won't have to be conscious of how far back you turn. Your windup will stop at the proper time, because you instinctively don't want to punish your muscles.

I'm sure you're saying to yourself right now that windup is really tension, and you've always heard how important it is to keep tension out of your golf swing. True, when it's tension occurring at the wrong time and place that inhibits movement. Windup is not that kind of tension. Rather, it's a tautness or stretching in the big muscles that is created as you move in a way you can react to. It's not a tightening but a state of elasticity that actually induces rather than stifles movement.

As the shoulders rotate on the backswing, the muscles in the left side of the back lengthen and become taut. It is this tautness that stops the coiling of the shoulders—actually before the backswing has been completed, as I pointed out —and induces a start in the opposite direction. The rubber band theory of stretching and snapping back is an over-simplification, because muscles do not really act that way, but for the purposes of understanding, the analogy is good enough.

It is this instinctive reaction that causes the forward swing. Why, you may ask, does this cause the left leg to lead the downswing, driving laterally toward the target? Why does not the upper body simply spin back around like a top, causing the arms and club to be spun counterclockwise on a similar path?

Let's first look at the lower body. The term "lower body lead" implies that the lower body unwinds first. It does not. But it is closer to the target and because it has not been pulled around as much as the upper, it only *looks* like it is going first. When the forward swing begins the lower body steals the show visually.

More specifically, if you have wound properly early in the swing, your back muscles get fully wound before your hands have reached the top of the swing. Remember, the hands are taking a longer route to get there. Therefore your shoulders are still under the influence of the centrifugal force that is carrying your arms, hands and club around. They are not free to move in the opposite direction, even though they might want to. Your lower body, however, is not under the

16. WHY MUSCLE WINDUP INDUCES RECOIL

Windup created by an early move of the left shoulder is illustrated here by the workings of the muscles in the upper left side and back. As the shoulders turn around the axis, these muscles are stretched to a point of tautness, wound so intensely that you cannot hold them in that position at the top of your backswing. Your body wants instinctively to recoil to alleviate their tautness. This instinct is stronger than your normal anxiety to hit with the right side. The involuntary reaction to this stretching helps start the forward swing.

influence of this centrifugal force and is free to move.

That, of course, explains why the lower body *looks like it* is moving forward before the backswing has been completed, while the club is still moving around behind you. This really is what happens, even though the impulse that is causing this forward move has come from the instinctive need of the shoulders to unwind and *not* from a *conscious* movement of the legs.

In the good players who make this move I notice that while the lower body moves forward early in relation to the backswing, it does not go left quickly. It moves slowly at first, almost like a slight lean toward the target until the upper body, arms and club begin to catch up with the lower. That's why I warned you not to try to make the move consciously. The whole sequence is so delicately and naturally timed that any effort on your part to make it work will disrupt it (see illustration #16).

There are other reasons why the forward swing reacts as it does. First, your mind is focused on the target. This attunes your lower body and your arms to go toward that target. If your mind and body were not pre-programmed to strike the ball in a certain direction, your body might simply go limp at the top of your backswing. It is the target that provides the motivation, while the initial movement of the left shoulder sets up the proper sequence of events in the swing.

That sequence is obviously rotational in nature. Your shoulders rotate at right angles to the spine on the backswing, so the return on the forward swing must have that same rotational shape. Even though the initial forward movement of the lower body is lateral, toward the target, it is followed by a counterclockwise turning motion of the legs and body. Finally, as the power of the right side is released at impact, there is a complete turn into the follow-through. You need not be concerned with it, because it will happen if you let it. But how is the club, in the midst of all this rotation, swung straight out toward the target?

The answer is that it isn't. The clubhead, too, is traveling in a rotating path around your body. Its proper route on the forward swing is from inside the target line to down the line to back inside again. But, in the properly timed swing, during the brief time that it is traveling down the target line at the bottom of its arc, it has struck the ball toward the target.

The clubhead is able to make that precise, on-line contact because it is being returned through the ball from a position *behind* you, from a point on or below the backswing plane instead of above it. As I've pointed out, if it started the return swing from above the normal plane, there is very little that could happen except a cutting action across the ball from outside to inside.

A word here about that plane and what is happening to it at the point when the backswing moves into the forward swing. As your upper body reaches its state of maximum windup and the lower body begins its forward movement, your club will drop even lower and farther behind you. This happens because this forward movement of the lower body has changed the balance point in your body. Your swing plane simply drops lower than it was on the backswing. This is what happens in the swings of the great players and is the inevitable result of a correct golf swing. This also puts the right side in a position farther behind the left as you move into the forward swing. This creates a position of leverage that instinctively subordinates the right side until your swing nears impact with the ball.

If you're a player of any experience, you may have noticed that I've said nothing about controlling the clubface. Nor do I intend to. Controlling the clubface implies manipulation of the hands, and that's the last thing I want you to think about.

The interesting thing is that while the arms and hands go in one direction and the body has begun to move in another, the clubface is very much in control because this swing does not violate any of the four fundamentals.

When the left side is leading, in control of the swing, there will be no flailing or rebounding of the clubhead at the top. It's the activity of the hands, specifically the right hand, which causes clubhead flail at the top. If you begin winding up early your hands will be too passive, too quiet at the top to interfere. Hogan looked like a whip, the unwinding of his lower body before the finish of his backswing putting a perceptible bend in the club at that point.

To put it another way, flailing is caused by uncocking the wrists too soon. But if the right elbow has moved underneath and closer to the body, as happens with proper lower body lead, the right wrist won't uncock and cause that flail. So control of the clubhead itself at the top is really not a conscious act in this system. The controlling factors are the existence of an axis, a plane that enables you to get back to the ball from inside rather than outside the target line and the maintenance of a radius through lack of right-side pressure.

For the same reason, I haven't mentioned what happens to the relative position of the arms and clubface in the backswing. They will rotate during the backswing, but this is a natural movement that need not concern you if you are

A

B

controlling your swing by starting it with the left shoulder. Unless you make a conscious manipulation of the arms and hands, your old friends axis, radius and plane will take care of everything quite nicely.

Let's quickly review what you've done so far in your golf swing. You've established *left-side control,* because you've subconsciously governed the golf club with your left side if you've started the swing with your left shoulder. You've kept that left-side control by fixing your axis, directing and maintaining your radius and achieving the maximum windup early enough to keep the left side in an advantageous position over the right. You've induced an *early left-leg drive* as a reaction to that maximum windup, and you've created a plane that has the club in a good position from which it can be swung through the ball on-target and with maximum speed.

How is that maximum speed achieved? By the simple fact of the body pulling the arms and the arms pulling the clubhead. The wrists merely act as a hinge, and the wristcock is maintained until the buildup of centrifugal force in the

17. WHAT HAPPENS IN THE FORWARD SWING

This series of drawings will give you a picture of what happens in the forward swing as a result of starting your swing correctly. A) The shoulders have finished turning before the hands reach the top of the swing, which is allowing the player to get a full windup. It is quite apparent from this view that the player has maintained both his radius and his axis on the backswing. B) On the forward swing the left leg leads and provides a platform that is maintained throughout the forward swing. The wrist only acts as a hinge as the lower left side leads the arms, hands and club into the hitting area. C) Here all the power of the right side has been allowed to release because

C

D

the left side has correctly led the forward swing. Note that the left leg continues to provide a platform for the swing. The right shoulder turning under the head shows that the swing has been properly guided by the four fundamentals. D) The body is turning into a full and free follow-through with the stomach facing the target. The arms have swung more around than up. Note the characteristic deep left knee-flex indicating that the left leg has not been straightened by pressure from the right side. All of the things described in these illustrations are results and are only pictured here to give you some idea of what happens in the forward swing. You should not deliberately try to copy any of these moves or positions.

clubhead begins the uncocking and brings the clubhead into the ball at maximum speed. It is this which causes the ball to come shooting off the clubface on the low trajectory which I consider most desirable.

This can only happen if the left side remains ahead of the right until the last possible moment before impact. Let's see how this is accomplished.

As you move into the ball, the left side is leading, pulling your arms and the club. The right side is not being used at all. Your lower body has shifted laterally but your head has not because the right shoulder is lowered and turns under it, keeping it in a relatively stable position.

By winding the upper body early and allowing the lower to react reflexively, you create the release of power at the proper time.

Eventually, centrifugal force of the swinging clubhead causes the wrists to uncock and brings the entire right side into play, producing that final explosion of power. The arms will rotate easily and correctly as they swing forward. The club will meet the ball with the back of the left wrist in a slightly bowed position resulting in a shot with low trajectory.

You don't have to worry about all these mechanical actions, because at this moment in a free, unrestricted swing all you're doing is holding onto the club. Anything you could do to help or hinder the shot has been done before.

There are a couple of trademarks of this swing that you can watch for. One is that your left knee will stay flexed a little longer because the left leg has moved forward early and is not being pressured and straightened by the right leg and hip. The other is a full and free follow-through. The fact that the right side has been properly activated late in the forward swing produces great extension of the arms through the shot, down the target line and on into a completely uninhibited follow-through (see illustration #17).

You see a lot of players, from poor to good, who follow through *upward.* That's because their shoulders are dictating that they move that way. But because you're turning freely through the shot as I talked about earlier, your momentum will carry you on *around* into a flatter finishing position with your upper body facing the target and the club in a near-horizontal position behind your left shoulder and head. The next time you get a chance, watch Lee Trevino, who has been accused of looking baseballish at the follow-through. That's because he hasn't blocked out anything. His whole right side is delayed so long and then allowed to release so freely and beautifully that it is whipped around and used completely and unguardedly in the follow-through.

Not only will you get around into that position, but you'll get there fast. It's been said that Hogan's swing from impact to finish was the quickest of any, and there's little reason to doubt it. That's because he had the entire right side going at that point in a completely uninhibited manner.

What I have done to this point is give you a close look at the golf swing, position by position, telling you what happens in each position and what each accomplishes. I want you to understand these positions as an aid toward achieving that clear, total concept of the swing. *Then I want you to put them out of your mind. Position is the last thing I want you to be concerned with when you get ready to make a golf swing.*

What I want you to think about is a *swing,* one that you can make freely and unguardedly without fear of hooking or slicing, pushing or pulling or any of the other mis-hit shots which plague most players. You can be sure of this because at the top of your backswing, that critical exchange point where most swings are destroyed, your stronger, dominant right side is not going to leap in and overpower the left.

You have no worries at that point, because the battle was won—or lost—long before. There is never a time in a Hogan-type swing, a Trevino-type swing, when there is so much as a standoff between the left and right sides. The left has assumed control at the start of their swings, as it will in your swing, by the simple expedient of starting that left shoulder forward.

Once this kind of authority is incorporated into your golf swing and it becomes a reflex action, you can forget about the rest of the swing. Everything else will happen correctly.

A word of advice here for the good player who is not attuned to thinking of the shoulder. Maybe you don't want to make the sacrifice of changing your thought. Maybe you like the way you're playing at the moment or you don't have enough time to practice and revamp the mental structure of your game. You should understand this concept, anyway. You may not realize it, but you're successful because you *do* make this movement at some time during the takeaway. I haven't seen any low-handicappers who don't turn the shoulder reasonably early. Knowing this at least will keep you from working on things that are detrimental to this movement when you get in trouble with your swing, as we all do at times.

That's why I never refer to this as *my* method. Almost all good players make this move instinctively. Some of them don't do it early enough in the swing, and very few of them do it habitually by turning instead of tilting the shoulders around the spine. Learning to do it immediately and in the proper direction can bring about dramatic improvement even in the skilled player.

Even more dramatic results can be gotten by the poor player or the beginner who has no concept of how the golf swing works and is confused over the right method of making it work. If you fit this description, this system is for you most of all.

CHAPTER FOUR: HOW TO PREPARE FOR THE MOVE

I liken the start of the golf swing to the start of a race—a mental and physical preparation, a sensing of the takeoff and the instant in which everything goes. In other words, "Get ready, get set, go!"

What actually happens in a golf swing is vitally important, of course, because it determines how you strike the ball. In my opinion, how you prepare for the shot is equally important, because it determines how you make the swing.

It involves how you hold the club and how you stand to the ball. The grip is the only link your body has with the club. An incorrect grip can throw up roadblocks to an effective swing. Your stance is the base on which your swing is made. Your posture determines your readiness to swing and how effectively your swing plane returns the clubhead along the target line. Your aim and the alignment of your body determine the direction in which you will strike the ball.

Most teachers feel these are vital elements in the golf swing. I agree. But in my opinion, the single, most important, and perhaps the most neglected, factor in making a successful swing is the way you prepare to make it. The routine which leads up to that swing should be an easy, graceful procedure which puts all the fundamentals properly to work and gives the swing a running start.

That routine includes another ingredient that often is overlooked. All successful shotmakers identify their target and have an ability to project the next shot to that target. Target projection and a repetitive procedure that takes you smoothly into the start of the swing will greatly improve your ability to make a golf swing that is effective and consistent.

In this chapter I'll explain how to make these preparations and their interrelationship. This will give you a foundation that makes the one move with the left shoulder an effective method with which to strike the golf ball and will tell you how best to bring that move into play.

GRIP

The best grip is one in which the two palms are facing, with the back of the left hand and the palm of the right hand facing the target. This allows the two hands to work together rather than in opposition to each other (see illustration #18).

This, in the idiom of golf instruction, gives you a "weak" grip. It really isn't weak, nor does it feel that way. It simply means that when your left hand is closed properly on the club, and you close your left eye, you can see only one knuckle. This means that the back of the left hand is facing

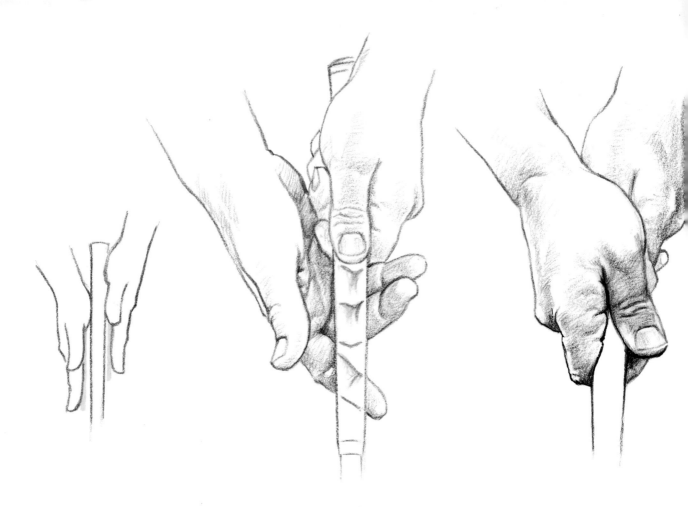

down or square to a line parallel to the target line.

This is an advantage for a couple of reasons. First, there is less chance of picking up the club on the backswing, less chance for the left hand to act as a lever. Secondly, in making any swing, whether you are striking a golf ball, beating a rug or slapping somebody backhanded across the face, your hand instinctively will return in a flat position at the moment of impact. When the hand is turned too far over to the right, you can see two or three knuckles. If you swing with this grip you must make some sort of compensation to keep the hand from returning instinctively where it wants to—in a flat or square position which would shut the clubface at impact.

With the left hand in the one-knuckle or square position, there can be a freer release of the right side into the shot, because even if the right side gets into the act a little early there will be less chance that you will hook the ball.

Also, when your left hand is facing the hole at address, it enables your whole left side to "hang" better from the shoulder and be more relaxed. Your left wrist will be "higher" or slightly arched, enabling you to put your right hand on the club in such a way that your right side is moved lower and made free of tension. This way not only the left shoulder but the whole upper torso will be able to move better.

You may find it difficult at first to play with the grip in this position. It's possible to play well with the left hand turned slightly more clockwise, but the one-knuckle position is ideal

18. PALMS FACE EACH OTHER IN PROPER GRIP
In a proper grip, the right palm should be facing the left palm as much as possible. This allows the two hands to work together, rather than in opposition to each other. When the right hand is closed, the left thumb fits into the fold of the right palm. The right thumb should be kept on the left side of the shaft in a harmless position.

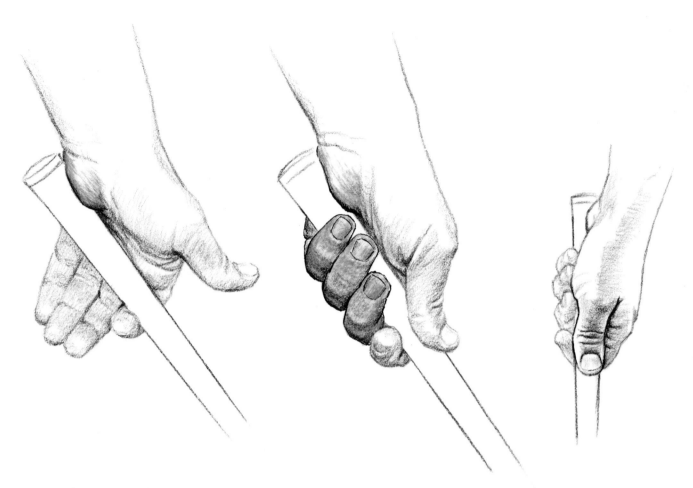

19. HOW TO ASSUME LEFT-HAND GRIP

To assume the left hand grip, the club is placed under the heel pad, running diagonally across the callous pads to the base of the forefinger (left). The last three fingers are closed then around the club. The forefinger should be slightly triggered. This allows the thumb to run straight down the shaft in a "semi-short" position (center), that helps secure the club. The back of the hand should approximately face the target (right).

for the system in this book.

Let's begin with your left hand. Place the handle of the club in the palm of the hand. It should rest underneath the heel pad and run on somewhat of a diagonal across the callous pads down to the base of your forefinger (see illustration #19). Now curl your forefinger around the handle. Without closing the last three fingers, lift the club and see if you can support it with your left forefinger and heel pad. If the shaft is too far down in your palm or not far enough under the heel pad, it will tend to slip and turn. If it remains solidly in place, you have it in the correct spot.

Now close the last three fingers, "triggering" or separating the forefinger slightly. You should feel that the club is controlled by a combination of the palm and fingers.

Assuming the grip in this manner, especially with the forefinger triggered, places your thumb on the club in a position I call a "semi-short thumb." It is not severely arched (don't make an effort to pull it up), but neither is it pushed down into an elongated position, lying flat against the club. There should be a small hollow spot underneath the base of the thumb. When the thumb is elongated, pushed down too flat, it sticks down into your right palm too far. This places too much bulk in that area, making it difficult for the right hand to be placed in a good position.

I advocate the "semi-short thumb" because it gives you a slight pressure between the thumb and forefinger and helps to secure the club. You should now have it secured three

20. HOW TO ASSUME RIGHT-HAND GRIP

In assuming the right-hand grip, the club is laid across the lower joints of the middle and ring fingers, as shown above, not across the callous pads as shown below. When the fingers close, the club should be lying snugly against the callous pads.

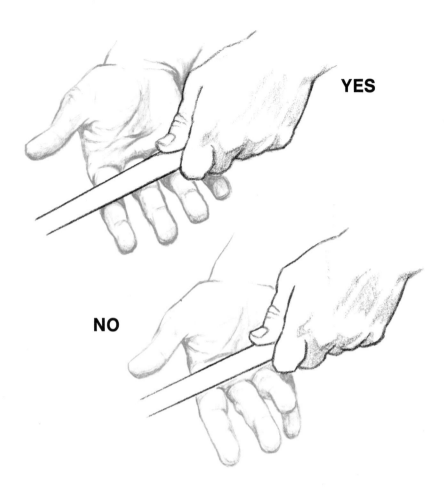

YES

NO

ways—with a downward pressure of the heel pad, an upward pressure of the last three fingers and the pincer pressure of the thumb and forefinger.

I prefer that the left thumb be placed on top of the shaft. I feel this helps keep the back of the hand facing the target. But some players find that difficult to do. It's not particularly detrimental to have it slightly on the right side of the handle, so if it fits better into your right palm in that position, go ahead and put it there.

When you're taking your left-hand grip, the club should be out in front of you in much the same position in relation to your body in which it will be at address. This insures that the hand will be placed correctly on the club in proper orientation to the body.

When placing the right hand on the club, it's important that the club be laid approximately across the lower joints of the middle and ring fingers. When the fingers close, the club should be lying snugly against the callous pad of the hand. In the Vardon grip, which I recommend, the little finger is hooked around behind the first joint of the left forefinger. If your fingers are short, it can ride piggyback on top of that joint (see illustration #20).

You should not separate the right forefinger too much from the other fingers. This "trigger" position creates an unwanted pressure on the forefinger.

21. YOUR COMPLETED GRIP SHOULD LOOK LIKE THIS

Your completed grip should look something like the two views shown here. Note the right thumb and forefinger in the harmless position on the left side of the shaft. The little finger of the right hand is hooked around the first joint of the left forefinger in the Vardon grip I prefer. However, both a ten-finger grip—with all ten fingers on the club—and an interlocking grip—with the left-forefinger and little finger of the left hand interlocking—are acceptable.

At this time, make sure that the left thumb fits into the fold of the right palm and the right palm is facing the left palm. Those are the two checkpoints to watch.

The position of the right thumb is extremely important. It should be virtually off the handle, hanging over on the left side with only the inside of the thumb touching the club. I call this the harmless position, because it discourages you from instinctively pinching the club with your right thumb and forefinger and applying pressure that can damage your swing (see illustration #21).

You should hold the club in both hands as lightly as possible. Relaxation is paramount in the golf swing. This is just another of the many times I'll remind you of that. If you hold the club too tightly your shoulders will be tense. This will make them hard to start, with the result that you will tend to take the club away with your arms and hands first.

Many golfers, particularly inexperienced ones, are afraid that if they hold the club too lightly they will lose control at the top of their swing. That doesn't happen, whether you're a weight-lifter or a weak old lady. Your grip will instinctively tighten the proper amount as you swing the club away.

If you have a correct grip, the only time the club will move in the left hand is when the right side takes over and hits too soon. That's what jars the club from your left hand. And, if that happens you will lose control of the club no matter how tightly you are grasping it.

It's easy to let yourself squeeze the club and tighten your muscles. It's difficult to convince yourself to be passive and graceful, holding the club lightly while preparing to strike the ball. You may need to work on this.

STANCE

The stance, or position of your feet, should be square. That is, both feet should be the same distance from the target line. I don't like to see the right foot in front of the left in an open stance because that puts the right leg in a dominant position. This creates leverage that can activate the right side too easily. This would cause the hips to turn and spin on the forward swing. It's better to have the right leg in a more passive position, square with the left (see illustration #22).

Your feet should be as wide apart as possible and still allow you to easily turn your shoulders. This will depend on your body flexibility. If your stance is too narrow, it could make you wobbly and prone to rotate your hips too early. As a general rule, your feet should be shoulder-width apart, measured from the inside of the heels, on a driver shot. They get progressively narrower as the clubs get shorter.

Your feet should be placed naturally, as they are when you walk. If your right foot splays out when you walk and you try to set it square—perpendicular to the target line—or toed in, it might offer resistance on the backswing, tense the lower right side and promote a tendency to hit from the top.

The left foot may be turned slightly more toward the target than it normally is inclined to be. This gives you an open feeling, not an open position at address. I'll discuss the advantages of this in a moment.

POSTURE

I mentioned earlier that posture has a lot to do with your readiness to swing. Proper weight distribution contributes a great deal to that readiness.

Your weight should be equally distributed between your feet. There is no need to try to put the weight on the insides of your feet to prevent swaying, unless that's the way you stand naturally. Maintenance of that vertical backswing axis will keep your weight from moving to the outside of the right foot.

Your weight should be toward the balls of your feet—not on the balls solely but somewhere between the arches and the balls. At the same time, your knees should be comfortably flexed. Your buttocks should protrude slightly and your

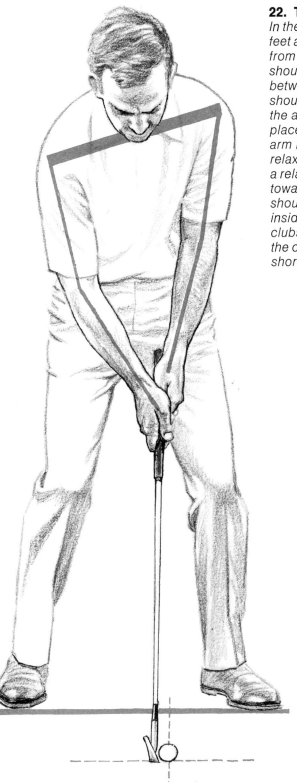

22. THE CORRECT STANCE

In the stance I recommend, the feet are square (the same distance from the target line). Your weight should be equally distributed between your feet. The right shoulder is lower than the left by the amount that the right hand is placed lower on the club. The left arm is relatively straight but relaxed and the right arm hangs in a relaxed manner, more folded in toward the right side. The ball should be positioned just off the inside of the left heel on longer clubs and moved back toward the center of your stance with shorter clubs.

lower spine be kept straight. There should be little or no tension in the small of the back (see illustration #23).

This position puts you in good balance. It puts a slight but healthy tension in the inner thighs that brings an alertness, an alive, catlike feeling to your lower body. It's as if you're ready to respond to a signal, and sure enough that signal will come, as you already know.

The amount you flex your knees depends in large part on your physical makeup. If you have short arms, you may need to flex your knees more to lower yourself to the ball. If you have difficulty starting the upper body before the lower, it may be helpful to flex your knees more than you do normally, squatting like a runner getting ready to start. But never flex to the point that your knees are protruding past your toes because this tends to make your legs loose and sloppy.

How erect you are—the tilt of your spine in relation to the ground—depends on the relative length of your arms and legs. There are other factors you must consider. Your arms should be relaxed and hang naturally. Bend over just enough to keep your weight toward the balls of your feet.

Within these guidelines, I'd prefer that you keep your upper body as erect as possible. The club will follow the lead of the shoulders and the shoulders turn at right angles to the spine. Thus, the more tilted or bent over your spine, the harder it is to turn them. The more erect you stand, the easier it is to turn your shoulders.

A player with a flat swing plane can be in trouble, of course, if he has a twirling action with the shoulders and does not have an early movement of the lower body. But you won't because your early upper-body windup and the subsequent forward reaction of your lower body will cause your left side to move first. Your right will not catch up until it is supposed to—at impact. You're gaining a tremendous advantage of leverage because of the forward-swing response you've created.

I mentioned that I want the lower part of your body in a position of catlike readiness and your torso as erect as possible. I don't want you to be ramrod stiff, however. If you let tension creep into your back and trunk, your torso will have that much more trouble turning. So stand with your upper body erect but quiet and relaxed, with your grip pressure light.

Your shoulders, arms and hands should hang in as relaxed and natural a state as possible. You will have to adjust your arms slightly to give them clearance from your body. You don't want to crowd the ball. If you feel too close to the ball when you start your left shoulder, you might instinctively rebel against allowing your arms to be swung out down the line. If your arms are extended just far enough from your body to allow clearance, you will be less reluctant to let them go where the shoulder directs them. As we have seen, allowing your shoulders to direct your arms is vital to this method.

Keep the lower portion of your back straight and your stomach tucked in. Then let your shoulders slump. You should be round-shouldered with a sunken chest. That part of your trunk should hang in an ape-like manner, totally relaxed. This induces a complete lack of tension that will allow your shoulders to move easily in starting your swing.

The right shoulder is lower than the left only by the amount that the right hand is lower than the left on the club. This helps relax your right arm and the upper right quadrant of your body. Forcing the right shoulder farther down in a misguided attempt to put it "under" in a more submissive position can restrict your radius. This would also prop the left shoulder too high, creating tension there that would make it difficult to initiate a good starting move (see illustration #22).

At this point, I'd like to dispute one of the precepts that golfers have lived by for years, the one that tells you your left arm must be straight at address. On the contrary, I'd prefer that your left arm be the way it naturally hangs at your side, relaxed and ready to respond to the movement of the shoulders. If your left arm is ramrod straight, it's likely to be rigid and tense. This can activate the arms too soon and force the club outside your natural swing plane before the shoulder has a chance to work.

So keep the left arm limp at address and let it be directed back where the shoulder wants it to go. The turning movement must create momentum that extends your radius and keeps the left arm as straight as you want it throughout the swing, maintaining your radius and allowing you to return the clubhead properly to the ball.

For the same reason—to avoid tension—don't try to draw the right elbow in close toward the belt in what you might think is a subordinated position. Just let the right elbow hang there, pointing just outside your right hip.

As viewed from the side, your left hand-forearm angle should be relatively straight at address. That is, the top of the left wrist should be in a fairly straight line with your forearm and hand. Certainly, it should not be in a sunken or

23. CORRECT POSTURE AT ADDRESS

Your posture at address contributes to your readiness to swing. The feet are square but the shoulders are open to the target line. This helps induce the early left shoulder start. The knees are well-flexed, indicating the weight is toward the balls of the feet, but not past the point of the toes. Have the feeling that the lower back is straight. The buttocks will protrude slightly. The shoulders are rounded and relaxed. The arms hang relaxed but far enough out to clear the body. The upper body should be erect but quiet and relaxed.

concave position.

You should not try to get the club into a straight-line position with your forearm. That will put you into an excessively arched, tension-filled position. The proper grip, arm-hand relationship and posture will insure that your club is set as it should be.

I would like to take issue with another of golf's bromides—that your hands must be ahead of the clubhead at address. The implication is that having the hands ahead previews the impact position, in which your hands and forearms ideally are leading the clubhead through the shot. In my opinion, this so-called preview has no significance. The instinct to hit with the right side is so strong that the clubhead will come in before the hands anyway if you don't make a good swing. You can put your hands forward and preview that impact position all you want, but if you don't load the gun well, you're going to hit with the right side.

To me, having the hands forward hinders loading that gun. The hands are the villains of the backswing. When they are forward at address they are in a position where they feel strong. They are more likely to move too soon. Also, the right arm and hand of most players are excitable to begin with. When the hands are forward the muscles in the upper right arm and shoulder tend to tighten even more. That just invites the right side to jump in and take the club away. At best, that tension will prohibit your arms from going where the upper left side directs them to go. It will restrict a correct turn of the right shoulder.

The hands instead should be in what I call the "neutral" position, preferably in the middle of your crotch and certainly no farther forward than the inner part of your left thigh. There I feel they are more relaxed, more passive, more receptive to having the shoulder start them back.

Don't change the position of the hands with different clubs. There is no need to move the hands ahead except on short shots, where you deliberately want to mimic the impact position because you don't build enough windup to achieve a left-side lead. More about that in Chapter 5.

The last, but certainly not the least important, portion of your anatomy to consider in correct posture is your head. It should be in the center of your stance, neither leaning one way or the other. It should be held high enough that your chin doesn't interfere with your shoulders when they turn. Your chin should be straight or cocked slightly to the right of the ball. You should view the ball with your left eye. You'll find this will give you more of a left-side awareness, making you better able to sense the movement of the left side and facilitate the backswing turn.

AIM AND ALIGNMENT

I've lumped together the two categories of aim and alignment because, while distinct, they certainly are interrelated. Aiming deals with the position of your clubface in relation to the target; alignment has to do with the position of your body in relation to both the clubface and the target.

Aiming the clubface is not as difficult as some make it. But it's where many players come to their downfall before they ever get started. Aiming the clubface means lining up the leading edge or bottom line of the club perpendicular or square to your target line. The reason this is not as simple as it sounds is that the position of your body, your head and eyes in relation to the ball and the target can create optical illusions.

To recognize correct clubface aim, assume your proper address position. Then have your professional or a friend stand behind the clubhead and adjust it so it is square on target. This might look strange to you at first. It probably will look as if the clubface is closed or facing left of the target. But as you strike practice shots with the clubface in this position, you will come to trust it as being correct.

The next step is to build your body alignment in relation to the clubface. Your feet actually have very little to do with alignment. The position of your shoulders and hips in relation to the target line is much more important (see illustration #24).

I want to explain the terms "open" and "closed." You are open when a straight line drawn from shoulder to shoulder (or across your hips) points generally to the left of your target. You are closed when the same line points to the right of the target.

It's better to aim your clubface before you align your body. The common fault is to do it the other way around, which usually results in your body being aligned on-target and your clubface aimed way to the right of it.

Aiming your club to the right of target, even though you may not realize it, creates all kinds of problems. You sense you're facing way to the right of the target. This inhibits starting your left shoulder around because you instinctively feel it's already partially turned.

At the same time, you'll feel a subconscious urge at the top of the backswing to use the right side to turn yourself back on target, to pull the ball around to the left. Once you

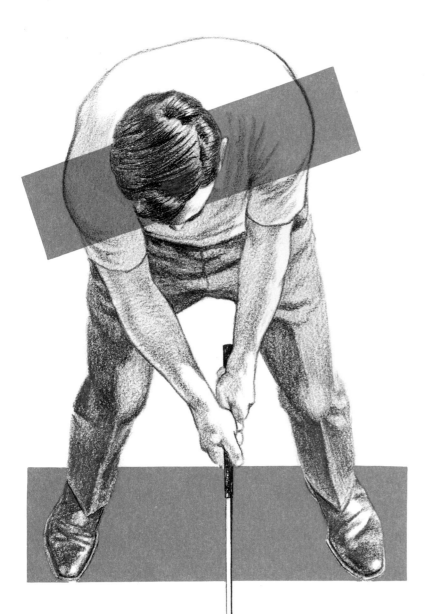

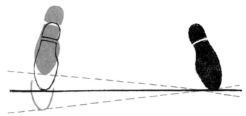

24. AIM AND ALIGNMENT

First, aim the clubface at your target. You can check this by lining up the leading edge of the clubface so that it is perpendicular to the target line, as shown here. Then align your body with the clubface. Your feet should be square to or equidistant from the target line. The outlined feet at right show differences between a square stance (both feet on the solid line), an open stance (right foot closer to the target line) and a closed stance (right foot drawn farther away from the target line). I recommend that the shoulders be open to the line of the feet at address. This open alignment makes you more aware of the target and encourages an early start by the left shoulder.

activate that right side, you'll tend to "come over the top." Worse, you inhibit a good early move with the lower left side because you have, in effect, blocked yourself out with that closed-shoulder position.

Even if, by some miracle of strength or will, you defeat the right side and manage to make a good swing, you'll obviously hit the ball to the right of your target. That's the way you were aiming in the first place.

Ideally, then, you should line up with your shoulders in an open position. A position square or parallel to the target line might be satisfactory, but an open position is even better. (I'm not going to have you worry about your hips here. If your feet and knees and your shoulders are aligned correctly, your hips will be, too.) I'd like to have you about 15-20 degrees open. You may want to work toward that point gradually, but that should be your goal.

This open alignment induces you to make an uninhibited start with the shoulder. The reason is that from a closed position you feel as if you can't turn fully without turning too far away from the target. An open position, on the other hand, gives you the feeling that you can turn fully. The open alignment also gives you a heightened awareness of the shoulder area to be moved. You get the feeling of more width to your swing, because you have a sense of the arms and hands swinging back farther along the line before they begin to swing around behind you. You feel that the arms and hands are responding to the movement of the shoulders.

Earlier I explained that the initial forward movement of the lower body on the downswing caused a flattening of the plane and a change in the direction of clubhead path, making it return more from the inside of the target line. Because of this, starting from an open shoulder position better allows you to return the club down that target line instead of more abruptly inside to out. Finally, a more open position subconsciously induces a stronger move with the lower left side toward the target.

Stance square, shoulders open . . . the combination will result in the movement that gets your swing squarely on line.

BALL PLACEMENT

Generally, if your body is aligned parallel to the target line or only slightly open to it as we discussed in the preceding passage, the ball should be played just off the inside of the left heel for a driver shot. From there, move it back gradually for each shorter club to a point in the middle of your stance for the short irons. This will allow you to strike the ball a more descending blow as you swing the shorter, more lofted clubs. Because you are taking some loft off the club when you do this, you will produce the lower shot trajectory that I feel is desirable.

We are talking gradations of inches and fractions of inches. It's something you must determine for yourself on the practice tee. You can tell by how solidly you're striking the ball. If you're making solid contact and the ball is going left, you have positioned it too far forward in your stance. If it goes right, the ball is too far back. A few minutes experimentation should give you the correct position for each club.

TARGET PROJECTION

We now come to the most important part of this chapter, the routine you follow to prepare for the shot. First I want to deal with something that I feel is an absolute necessity for good play—*target projection.*

Target projection is visualizing where you want to strike the ball, the flight of the ball as it goes to that spot, and even where it lands and how it rolls. This visualization serves several important functions. It gives you a sense of what the shot requires and helps bring your instincts into play. It helps you align yourself properly. The mind is a computer. It won't let you get away with an improper address position. The mind always carries an image of the primary target. If you're on line, the computer checks it off and lets you make a good swing. If you're mis-aligned, you get a short circuit. The body is instructed to make a compensation during the swing.

Target projection will help trigger your shoulder move in the correct way. It sets your mind and body ticking in continuous and harmonious motion from the time you begin your setup procedure until you begin your swing. Thinking of the target instinctively assists you in starting the shoulder at the right time in your setup sequence.

Having a good picture of the target gives your muscles a feeling for the kind of shot you want to hit. If you disregard where you're trying to hit the shot, you're ignoring vital instincts.

Being conscious of the target keeps you from being too conscious of the ball and from thinking too long about starting the shoulder. The upper left side works best when it's started as a reaction to a glance at the target. Look at the target, then react by putting the club down behind the ball and starting the shoulder. Thus you won't dwell on the ball or on how to make the move. You will simply make the move better. I don't care how many times you look at the target . . . you may look, waggle, look, waggle, look to your heart's content, depending on the type of shot and other circumstances. But after you look at the target for the final time and put the club behind the ball, try to develop the feeling that the shoulder is going to start.

Once you get used to that kind of a routine, you won't stand over the ball and get tied up.

On full shots, don't try to visualize a target that is too far away. If you do, it will cause anxiety and a tightening of the muscles in the back and arms that will make it difficult for the shoulder to start promptly.

On short shots, target projection helps you govern the instincts of the arm-and-hand swing. On chip shots and putts you don't wind up to the point that the forward swing is a reflex; but picturing your target has a direct bearing on where you swing the club and how softly or hard you swing it.

SETUP PROCEDURE—YOUR ROUTINE

For some of you, this passage may be the most important in the book. If you think you can stand to the golf ball any old way and move the upper left side and be successful, you're going to be disappointed. The swing takes less than two seconds so there's no time for thinking. Everything that happens in the swing largely depends on what you do prior to its start.

In other words, get ready . . . get set . . . and go. But before you can go you must get ready and get set. I can't overemphasize the importance of this.

All good players have a routine that suits them. Make it a point, the next time you're at a professional tour tournament, to watch this facet of the stars' play. You'll never see Jack Nicklaus hit a shot without getting behind the ball, lining up the shot and approaching it in a certain manner. That's his routine. Bruce Crampton and Jerry Heard have a soft, subdued waggle. Sam Snead has a big waggle. So has Hogan. Each has his pattern and routine.

You see, it's easier to continue a motion than to originate it. That's why the start of the actual swing should be a continuation rather than a beginning motion. If you're standing statically over the ball, you will tend to think of too many unimportant things . . . whether you've made the right decision on the shot, chosen the right club, the importance of the shot.

Once you've made a decision on what you want to do with your shot, you should have a standard procedure, one which is ingrained into your muscle patterns so that you do it the same way every time. This routine should get you aimed and aligned properly, get the ball in the proper position in your stance, insure that your posture is correct, get your upper body supple, your right side relaxed and lead you immediately into the swing.

That's why a player like Lee Trevino performs so well under pressure. He has a consistent routine that carries him, even when he's nervous, from the moment he approaches the ball right through the act of making the shot. He has a definite, positive plan that takes care of his pre-shot preparations and puts him in the right frame of mind to execute the good move that starts the swing.

If you can develop such a routine, then ingrain it into your mind and body so it becomes a systematic action you can perform without much conscious thought, you'll be on your way to better shotmaking. You'll be able to direct your mind to the target which, as I explained, induces a much more effective swing. And you'll be able to better take that swing onto the golf course and make it work. Hitting the ball well on the practice tee is easy compared to making your swing work under actual conditions of play. But if you've developed a good rhythmical routine that instinctively triggers the start of the swing, you'll find yourself much better able to concentrate on playing the game and making a good score. I will have more to say about that in Chapter 6.

Good setup procedure, as I've discussed earlier, blends target projection, grip, aim, alignment, ball placement, stance and posture into a syrupy smooth pattern of movement that gets you ready to hit the shot. Each becomes interrelated with the other as you get prepared to start the left shoulder and begin your swing.

Having visualized your target, you must be subconsciously aware that you want to align your knees and feet parallel to the target line and your shoulders open. You can see the target better when you are facing it, and you can better relate to the target line. Many good players approach the ball in this manner. The shoulders should be open as the setup routine starts, which encourages you to keep them open as the setup routine continues.

If instead you make your approach from a point even with or ahead of the ball, you'll be starting with your shoulders parallel. The odds are that you'll close them to the target as you complete your setup, making it more difficult to make the correct starting move.

The first thing you do is set the club down in front of you

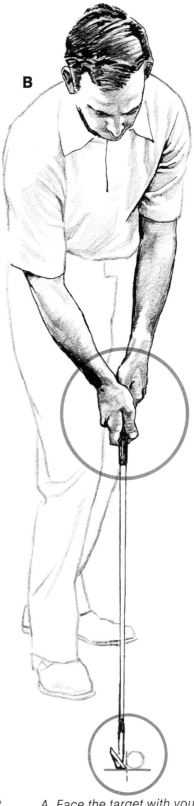

25. ALWAYS SET UP
WITH THE SAME ROUTINE

A routine setup procedure that never varies is a vital aid in starting your swing correctly. Here is an ideal routine to follow as you prepare to make a shot. First, place your left hand on the club in the correct position. Then step back and stand slightly behind the ball in the position shown in figure

A. Face the target with your weight on the left foot, your right foot pointing toward the target line. Next, step forward with the right foot as you place the club squarely behind the ball and simultaneously assume your right-hand grip as shown in figure B. Your right foot is closer to the target line now

C

D

than it eventually will be. Then, place the left foot into its correct address position relative to the ball and the target line, as shown in figure C. Finally, adjust the right foot into position (the same distance from the target line as the left) as shown in figure D, all the while keeping your shoulders

aligned open to or pointing left of the target line. The entire procedure should be made in a smooth, rhythmic sequence that will carry you, without tension, into the starting move of the left shoulder. As you take your final looks at the target, remain in motion, primarily by waggling.

in a normal address position and assume your left-hand grip. Then step back (see illustration #25). Your chest should face the target, with your weight on your left foot . . . your right foot forward toward the target line.

At this point, your left arm hangs limply at your side. Now step forward with your right foot, placing it down closer to the target line than it eventually will be. At the same time, place the clubface in position behind the ball. As you do this, put your right hand on the club in the proper position. Your right elbow should be hanging just an inch or two from your right hip after you do this.

You should practice to make these smooth, rhythmic, almost simultaneous movements. You want a precise, automatic sequence that swings your right side into a lower, relaxed position, ready to respond to the left side. Making the initial club-to-ball move with your left hand and arm will accomplish two things—you will instantly establish left-side control and you will measure the approximate distance you want to stand from the ball.

The next movement will be the placement of your left foot. Remember that the right foot is closer to both the target line and the ball than you want it, so the left foot will be placed farther from the target line than the right. As the left foot is placed, make sure the shoulders remain open. Then adjust the right foot, moving it both away from the target line and back from the target.

From this point on, your motion should not cease. As you take your final look or looks at the target, remain in motion primarily by waggling.

The waggle is a movement of the club away from and back to the ball, starting along the target line. It is done with the left arm and hand. Make sure the right does not get into the act at all, because it could then become prominent at the start of the actual swing.

The waggle serves to break tension which might occur should you remain static. The waggle should be made in a square to open manner. The left hand and arm roll slightly clockwise going back from the ball, then counterclockwise returning to it. That will be their natural movement in the swing itself. It may be a big waggle or a small one. Make as few or many as you wish. The important thing is that the waggle be natural and become automatic.

Even though we're concerned with getting the left shoulder started, don't waggle with the shoulders. This can make you very stiff and shoulder conscious, making it difficult to get started. It can also destroy your alignment.

I also coordinate my waggle with a slight, alternating up-and-down movement of my feet. I find this keeps my body from getting tight. If you can incorporate a similar movement into your routine, I think you'll be the better for it.

I do not recommend a forward press, even though it is a commonly accepted method of starting the swing. I feel that a forward press with the hands can get them into too strong a position that might create some tension in the upper right side, thus bringing it into play. A forward press with the knees or legs gets your lower body into motion. This tends to get it started too soon on the backswing, eliminating the necessary separation between upper and lower. If you already have a forward press in your routine, go ahead and do it, so long as it comes naturally. But I'd recommend that you try to minimize it, through practice, so it doesn't create either of the disturbing influences I mentioned.

Rather than use a forward press as the means to start your swing, simply take a look at the target and back to the ball, put the club down behind the ball for an instant and then *go.* For just a split second think "start the left shoulder forward" and the inertia will be broken. Don't set so long that you stop the rhythmic momentum of your routine. Let it carry over into the movement that starts your left shoulder.

When I'm under tension, probably on a key shot, when I feel the shoulder a lot at the start of the swing, I'm in trouble. I'm struggling with something that doesn't want to go. When I'm relaxed and doing my setup procedure well, I don't feel anything.

This entire routine should be gone through in a relatively brief period of time—five or six seconds, more or less, depending on your natural tempo. Developing this routine will take practice, patience and a gradual building of confidence in your ability to do it. But it is vital in making you a better player.

Let's review now the elements of setup procedure we've learned in this chapter. This list can be referred to whenever you run into trouble:

Grip. Club under the heel pad of the left hand, the forefinger curled around under the handle, the left thumb in a semi-short position, the back of the hand facing in the direction of the target. The club is placed in the right hand against the base of the callous pad of the middle and ring fingers. The little finger is hooked behind the left-hand fore-finger. The thumb and forefinger of the right hand are in a harmless position, the thumb hanging to the left with only its side touching the handle. The right palm is facing the left palm, which means the two hands are square or neutral. The grip is light and relaxed.

Stance. The feet are square to the target line, the inside of the heels about shoulder width apart for a driver shot, progressively narrower for the other clubs.

Posture. Your weight is equally distributed from side to side, toward the balls of your feet, your legs feeling alive and catlike. Your knees are flexed, your stomach tucked in, your buttocks slightly protruded, your lower spine straight. Your upper body is as erect as possible from the hips, but you assume a round-shouldered position, your arms hanging naturally, extended only enough to feel you have clearance of the body and are not crowding the ball. Your right shoulder is lower than the left only by the amount your right hand is lower than the left on the club. Your left arm is relaxed and slightly bent, your right elbow hanging naturally and pointing just outside the right hip. Your hands are centered about at your crotch, your hand-forearm angle relatively straight. Your head is in the center of your stance, chin straight or cocked slightly to the right and held high enough that it doesn't interfere with your shoulder turn.

Aim and Alignment. First, you face the target with the upper body. Then you aim the clubface so that the bottom line of your clubface is aimed perpendicular or square to the target line. Keeping your shoulders open, then align your feet and knees square to the target line.

Ball placement. In general, the ball is placed off the inside of the left heel for a driver shot and worked back gradually to a point in the middle of your stance for short irons. Two checkpoints are how straight and solidly you are striking the ball and its trajectory.

Target projection. Visualizing the target and the projected line of flight gives you a feel for the shot, helps you align properly and helps trigger the shoulder motion. On short shots it governs the instincts of the arm-and-hand swing. On long shots be careful not to visualize a target too far in the distance, because this will create tension.

Setup routine. Having taken your left-hand grip, stand behind an imaginary line drawn from the ball back to you, perpendicular to the target line, your weight on your left foot, your right foot forward perpendicular to the line as you face the target, your shoulders open, your left arm hanging limply at your side. Step forward with your right foot, place the club in position behind the ball and at the same time assume your right-hand grip. Place your left foot in position, make sure your shoulders remain open to the target line, adjust your right foot backward, and assume your correct posture. Continue motion with a square-to-open waggle, done with the left hand and arm away from and back to the ball, and with a slight movement of the feet. Take a final glance at the target, set the club for an instant behind the ball and start your left shoulder forward. The routine should be so ingrained that it becomes something you do rhythmically without conscious thought, a repeating systematic action that gives you no time to let extraneous thoughts interfere.

CHAPTER FIVE: APPLYING THE MOVE TO THE SHORT GAME

The early move with the left shoulder works with the short game, too. It can help you become a better putter than you thought possible. It can transform a sloppy chipping and pitching game into one that has confidence and consistency.

The problem with short shots is that because they seem to be such delicate operations, your impulse is to make the swing with the hands and arms only. This does nothing to subdue the right side. If you give the right side an even chance it's very likely to jump in and ruin the shot. That's because of two interrelated reasons:

1. The normal anxiety you have toward hitting any shot is magnified by the delicacy required on a short shot, so you have an urge to hurry into the forward stroke.

2. No matter how short the shot, you need some power, and you'll instinctively act to provide that power.

Both of these instincts will be satisfied by forcing with the right side unless you place it under control immediately by starting the swing with the left shoulder. This provides your power base.

The same fundamentals apply to the short swing, including the putting stroke, that apply to the full swing. We want to make sure the left side is ahead of the right on the return through the ball and that the arm and hand swing is coordinating with the movement of the body. It's simply the full swing in miniature. Obviously you don't create the full windup on putts or short shots that you do with the full swing. But you still must create immediate windup with an early shoulder move, because that provides the leverage that gives the left side the advantage.

The left shoulder move also sets up centrifugal force that gets the clubhead behind the hands. This is necessary in all swings, of course, but is more difficult to achieve in smaller strokes. Unless the clubhead is behind the hands on the forward swing, the left side cannot lead through the shot because it will not be in the proper position of leverage.

Your hands and upper body must be relaxed so your hands and arms can respond to the initial movement of the left shoulder. There should be no deliberate cocking of the wrists. The wrist cock is a natural result of the arms and hands being swung backward. On a very short chip, they will cock very little. On a half-wedge shot or more, they will cock almost fully. But this is nothing you consciously do.

Let's examine the fundamentals that will give us the short-shot swing that we want:

Your grip is the same as for the full shot. Your stance and body position should be more open, facing slightly to the left

26. STAND MORE OPEN ON SHORT SHOTS

On short shots, your stance should be more open, so that you face slightly more to the left of the target than for full shots. This allows you to sense your target better. For very short shots, your feet should be more open, about 40 degrees, than your shoulders, which should be about 25 degrees open. The fact that your shoulders are less open than your feet means that they are, in effect, already wound a little. This creates some separation even before you start the swing.

27. HOW THE STARTING MOVE WORKS ON SHORT SHOTS

Standing open works best for short shots because from this position you can turn your shoulders and create as much windup as you do on full shots (see illustrations below). This helps relieve the anxiety to bring the right side into play too early, a condition which is even more common on short shots than long ones. From an open stance, all you need to think about is starting the swing with the left shoulder, just as you do on full shots, and let the rest of the swing happen.

of the target line. For the shorter shots, your feet should be about 40 degrees open, your shoulders about 25 degrees open. When the length of the swing is such that you feel you must strain from an open position, return to the normal stance and alignment you use for the full swing (see illustration #26).

Your feet should be just wide enough apart to provide a solid base upon which to build your swing. This may be as little as three inches between the heels for the very shortest shots. If your stance is too wide, it tends to create tension, inhibiting the forward swing response.

The effect of your open stance and shoulder alignment is two-fold. First, you can sense the target better and more easily swing your arms out toward the target because you're facing it. Second, and more important, by the fact that your shoulders at address are squarer to the intended line of flight than your feet, you've in effect wound them a little before you start. This creates some windup before you begin and continues to create it as you swing back. The separation of the upper and lower body, one of the major factors of windup, is also given a head start from this open position. You will wind the back muscles more on short shots from this position than from a more orthodox, squarer stance. The additional shoulder turn helps relieve the anxiety to bring that right side into play (see illustration #27).

If you set up properly to this shot, you can feel a small amount of tautness in your upper left back. This is the beginning of windup. The feeling is not one of tension but rather one of security, a sense of having the swing under control.

Your position should remain basically the same as for the full swing, with two notable exceptions—you should squat or flex your knees more and your pelvis should not be tucked in as much. You do this because you want your upper body to remain erect. If it's bent over excessively, it's difficult for the shoulder to turn correctly, at right angles to the spine.

At the same time, the club is shorter and you're also choking down on it—I like to grip it down near the metal part of the shaft for better control on the little shots. You also want to play the ball closer to your feet so that club will tend to travel more on the target line back and through the swing. The best way I have found to satisfy all these requirements and still keep the arms relaxed is to squat, lowering myself to the ball. Your checkpoints must be to keep your pelvis tucked in, *but not as much as on the full swing,* and keep your lower back straight. Your weight should be balanced between the left and right feet and forward toward the balls of your feet. These factors will determine how much knee flex you need without your having to worry about it.

The ball should be played just inside the *right* heel for the shortest shots. Since the centerpoint of your weight is between your feet, the lowest point of your swing arc will fall at the same place. If you position the ball slightly behind that point it will insure that you strike the ball while the club is traveling a slightly downward path. In other words, you contact the ball first instead of catching the turf and ruining the shot.

Relaxation of the upper body, arms and hands is imperative. It cannot be stressed too much. This allows the arms and hands to be influenced by the movement of the shoulder, as I've said earlier. Conversely, if the arms and hands are tight, they will tend to move first on the backswing. If this happens on the short shot, you won't have enough time to get the shoulder going at all, leaving you at the mercy of what can happen when the arms and hands control the swing—they can pull your shoulder down, causing loss of axis, windup and plane, leading to mis-hits and crooked shots.

So relax and keep the left arm from getting rigid. It can be straight, but make sure it's not locked tightly into place.

A final word on separation. I hope by now I've convinced you of how important it is to move the upper body before the lower body at the start of your swing. On a very short shot, a chip from the fringe, *you need no lower body activity at all on the backswing.* On the half and three-quarter shot you need just a little. There obviously will be some lower body motion on the forward swing. But on the backswing the shoulder does not turn enough to pull the hips and legs around perceptibly. Now, I don't mean for you to keep them rigidly in place. Just concentrate on starting the upper left side first. That will create all the separation you need.

The short-shot swing will not be as automatic or reflexive as the full swing, simply because you are not creating as full a windup. But the impulse to hit the ball hard is subdued because you have put the right side in a subordinated position, which induces a proper left-side lead. Be aware of your shoulders turning and returning, your hands staying ahead of the clubhead or the back of your left hand going toward the target. Practice this. Become aware of what it feels like. When you get on the course, don't try to recreate it. Just let it happen.

An indication of a good short-shot swing is that the club accelerates through the ball on the forward swing. You don't want to swing haltingly, in wishy-washy fashion. Once you embrace this concept and practice it for awhile, you'll be able to make a smaller shoulder turn and a smaller backswing, thus increasing your control while still moving the clubhead crisply through the ball.

The best way to program a proper shoulder turn and backswing length is to take a couple of practice swings before every short shot. Look at your target and practice the arms-and-hands swing you instinctively feel you need to get the ball there. This builds a little muscle memory and will help you make a more reflexive swing when you actually hit the shot.

Here's an important point—do your thinking about distance needed and other factors *during the practice swing.* In making the shot, think only of the shoulder move, and then only for the split second that it takes to start it. As I explained earlier, thinking of the shoulder turn too long can retard the natural acceleration of your swing. It is especially important that you do not dwell on the turn in a short swing. If you do, you will consciously direct your backswing almost to its completion, which will rob your swing of its feel, instinctiveness, rhythm and momentum. Don't over-think!

Recall what I said in Chapter 2 about letting your instincts take over when it comes to distance and direction. If you've done everything well to that point, trust them and they'll work for you.

A question often asked me is, when do I chip (a low shot that runs) and when do I pitch (a high shot that stops more quickly)? Consider this: the farther you carry the ball onto the green with a pitch shot, the longer the swing you need and the greater the chance for error. The quicker you can get the ball back on the ground, the safer your shot will be.

A good rule of thumb is to carry the ball the first one-third of the distance to the flag, letting it roll the other two-thirds. Bear in mind, of course, that the ball ideally should land on the putting surface. On uphill or downhill shots, the formula changes. But if you follow the "one-third" rule and practice accordingly, you'll soon learn to select the club that will land the ball where it can roll the rest of the way to the hole.

When you make practice swings, you'll find it helpful to visualize the spot on which you want the ball to land rather than visualizing the flag itself. This has the effect of reducing a 45-foot shot to a 15-foot shot. A smaller swing is easier to relate to. You will feel the shot is less demanding and has less margin for error. This psychological effect will promote a better, more confident swing.

THOUGHTS FOR SPECIAL SITUATIONS

The condition of the turf greatly determines the amount of

backspin you'll get on your shot. When the ground is dry and the grass clipped reasonably short, you'll tend to get more backspin. If the grass is wet or you're lying in clover or nestled in thick-bladed grass, you'll get less backspin because the grass and moisture will get between the clubface and the ball, lessening the friction which causes spin.

To hit the ball low, move the ball back a couple of inches, choke down on the club and make a crisp accelerating forward swing. If you have to make an extremely low shot and stop it quickly, place the ball two inches to the right of your right foot. This will drastically de-loft the clubface and will force you to make an abrupt up-and-down swing. You'll produce a low-trajectory shot with a great deal of backspin. This is an effective shot in playing off bare dirt, because it virtually eliminates the chance of hitting behind the ball. Just make sure you keep your body open to the target and keep the blade square at address or you'll hit the shot to the right.

SAND PLAY

The shot from sand bothers most amateurs. It shouldn't, because you do not actually strike the ball but rather a spot two or three inches behind it. If you keep four important points in mind, the sand shot is easier than any other pitch shot.

First, on most sand shots the face of the club should not close as it cuts through the sand. This insures that the club slides smoothly through the sand, nicely lifting out the ball as it passes underneath it. When you address a normal sand shot, your clubface should be opened up a little. This provides added *loft* and backspin for the shot and helps prevent the clubface from closing and digging in.

To prevent closing the clubface and digging, I recommend that you move your grip at address to a "weaker" position just a fraction to the left of the neutral position I described in Chapter 4. Here is a way to move into that position without disrupting your normal gripping procedure. Open the clubface about 10 degrees more than you normally would. Assume your normal grip with the clubface in this position. Then close the clubface (rotate it counterclockwise) to the desired address position. Be sure not to change your grip as you rotate the club. This is a simple way to weaken your grip because you can use the grip you are familiar with. This makes you more comfortable and confident. (see illustration #28).

28. AN EASY WAY TO GET WEAK GRIP
To achieve a weaker grip for the sand shot without disrupting your normal gripping procedure, open the clubface about 10 degrees more than normal, as shown at left. Then simply place your hands on the club the same way you always do. Now, rotate your hands counterclockwise, as indicated at right, until the clubface is where you want it. This will put your grip in the desired "weak" position for the sand shot and you will have buffered the change in feeling.

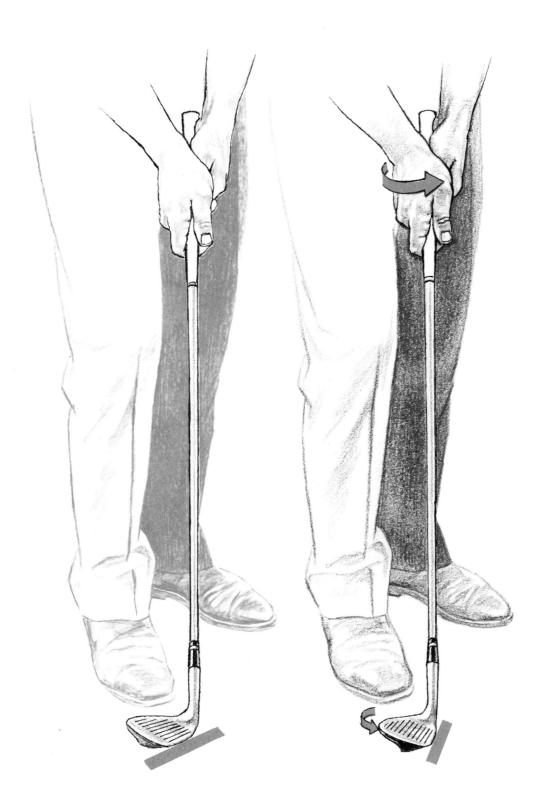

Second, I believe the sand shot should be made with fundamentally the same swing as any other pitch shot. Play the ball off the inside of your right heel. Aim your open clubface at the flag. Open your stance slightly more than for a pitch shot—about 45 degrees. Your shoulders should be about 35 degrees open. Then swing normally. There are no gimmicks or adjustments to make. Start the swing with the left shoulder. This causes the clubhead to travel on the same wide swing arc back and through as it does on full shots. Because you do not pick up the club abruptly and stab it down as some sand methods advocate, you'll take a shallower cut of sand. This allows a good follow-through. The result is more backspin and control over the ball, because you don't lose clubhead speed (see illustration #29).

Third, always try to strike the sand about two or three inches behind the ball. Address that spot and not the ball to aid eye-hand coordination. Vary the distance you need by the force of the swing. When you reach a point where even a full swing will no longer get you to the target, reduce the distance you hit behind the ball. On long sand shots, where you need a full swing and distance with a particular club, square your stance and square the blade. Grip and swing normally. On those longer trap shots, position the ball about the middle of your stance. You'll lead more with your body in the fuller swing and your weight will move more to the left.

Finally, before you make a sand shot, be sure you achieve a solid stance by grinding your feet in the sand until they're firmly settled. This also helps you determine the sand's texture and gives you an idea of how hard you must swing.

To be a competent bunker player, you must know what the texture of sand demands of your swing. In coarse or wet sand you must make an easier swing because the clubhead doesn't cut as deeply. Light, powdery sand dictates a more forceful swing.

You must practice to be a good sand player. Use the practice bunker at your own course on a regular basis to perfect the fundamental swing. Try always to hit a few sand shots before you play a strange course just so you'll know what you're getting into—and hopefully out of.

OUT-OF-THE-ORDINARY SAND SHOTS

Downhill. I must warn you that the method I have taught you does not work on a sand shot from a steep downhill lie. No normal method does. Instead, follow this procedure:

● Play the ball two or three inches to the right of your right toe. This will move your hands back to the vicinity of your

29. USE SAME SWING FOR SAND SHOTS
The sand shot swing is the same as any other. Aim the clubface at the target and stand very open— about 45 degrees with the feet and 35 degrees with the shoulders. This combination encourages good use of the flange on the bottom of your sand wedge which allows the club to ride smoothly through the sand. Simply start with the left shoulder and swing normally. This gives you the same wide swing arc back and through as it does on full shots. The result is a shallow and effective cut through the sand compared to the steep up-and-down action some methods advocate. Note the full, free follow-through, a trademark of this sand swing.

right knee, naturally causing your left shoulder to drop and your right shoulder to raise more.

● Move your left-hand grip into a stronger position by rotating it clockwise so you can see all the knuckles.

● Pick a target a little left of the flag to insure that the ball does not spin right of the hole. Align yourself only about 20 degrees to the left of that target line. Remember that because your hands are pulled back to the right your shoulders will be open even less than normal.

● Initiate the takeaway by immediately cocking the wrist and swinging the club on as upright an arc as possible. On the downswing, "pull" the club in the direction of your left knee to promote a steeper descent. A vertical swing is the objective here. But it should be done as slowly and rhythmically as possible.

Buried. Play the shot from a buried lie in sand the same as a low pitch shot from grass. Move the ball back a couple of inches, choke down on the club and make a crisply accelerating forward swing. You also should hood or de-loft the club. This forces the blade more deeply into the sand behind the ball. When a softer shot from a buried lie is required, an upright action with a quick wrist-cock more akin to the downhill-lie swing gets the job done.

PUTTING

The average golfer thinks golf's shorter shots are played with the hands and wrists, so somewhere down around the 8- or 9-iron he stops turning. Therefore it's not surprising that most golfers seldom, if ever, think about *swinging* a putter.

You should turn on all shots, even putts. On the green you have the same old problem of the right side taking over, pushing the putterface off line, or the right shoulder moving the head forward and destroying your axis. Starting the putting stroke with the left shoulder solves that problem just as it does in the full swing. The early shoulder move gives you better rhythm, more power with a shorter swing, more consistent speed on the ball and more chance to succeed under pressure because it allows you to keep the same swing thought from the drive to the putt.

You might ask why simply putting with the left hand and arm isn't good enough for such a small stroke. I've spent long hours taking the putter back with my left forearm, and it's always had a tendency to wobble. Starting the swing with the shoulder stabilizes the putterhead. The bigger muscles can control the direction it moves more easily than the hands and wrists. A little turn of the shoulder produces a lot of clubhead movement and more power than you would get by using the hands. So, you don't have to make up for any lack of power by trying to hit with the right. And, since you don't have to move the shoulder much, you avoid making the big backswing that usually causes instinctive deceleration on the forward stroke. Your forward putting stroke, like your full swing, becomes a reaction to a simple action. Starting the putter stroke with the left shoulder movement creates a swinging motion that lets you instinctively feel the same rhythm you get in a full swing. When putting with the arms alone, it is sometimes difficult to sense that rhythm.

The rhythmic use of the shoulders produces a more consistent swing and with it more consistent speed as the ball comes off the putterface. If the ball is coming off at the same speed every day, it won't take you long to figure out how far it's going to roll. You'll also be able to putt rolling greens better, because you can depend on the ball breaking more consistently in those situations where speed is such a factor.

I believe using the shoulders in putting helps you perform better under pressure. On the practice green where nothing matters and you're relaxed, almost anything works. An experienced player who has good nerves, a lot of confidence and doesn't back off from pressure can take fair mechanics and make them work. Billy Casper and Jerry Barber are examples of super putters who have wristy strokes. But they're gifted with good nerves. Most of us can't control ourselves that well under pressure.

When you activate the putter with your hands and arms, you don't have the consistency of grip pressure that you need. Usually your grip tightens, destroying both rhythm and clubface alignment. When you putt with your hands, especially under pressure, it is difficult to take the putter back far enough to hit the ball at the right speed. You're susceptible to rushing into the forward swing, thus cutting short your back swing and misdirecting the putt.

However, if your thought is directed toward starting the swing with your left shoulder, your hands merely are a passive part of the over-all motion and are much less likely to interfere. And it's much easier to keep the shoulder muscles relaxed during a tense situation, simply because they are bigger than the muscles in your hands.

The beauty of this putting method is that it applies to everybody, to beginners or experts. You don't need any special technical know-how.

That's the objective—to simplify, to get you down to a basic thought. Then, I'll warn you, you must repeat it over and over in practice. I think you'll improve immediately, but you'll never become as good as you can be unless you practice. There are no short-cuts. No system eliminates work.

There are certain fundamentals I feel you must incorporate with this basic thought to be a better putter. Let's take a look at them.

Grip

The purpose of the putting grip I advocate is to lessen the influence of the fingers, putting the club handle more in the palms of both hands. With the motivating action coming from the left shoulder, the more passive your grip, the better you'll putt (see illustration #30).

To this end, place the club diagonally across the heel pad of the left hand, not underneath the heel pad as in the full-swing grip. If it's under the heel pad, the fingers have too much control. You'll find that by laying the club across the pads, you take the fingers off the club to a great extent. Only the tips are on the grip. Your left forefinger is off the club completely, extending downward and lying on the fingers of the right hand. This is called the "reverse overlap" grip. Your left thumb goes on top of the shaft, running straight down.

In the right hand, the club rests in the base of the

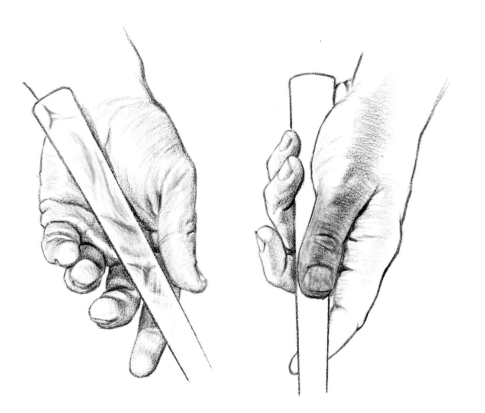

30. PLACE PUTTING GRIP
IN PALMS, NOT FINGERS

To lessen the influence of the fingers in putting, I advocate placing the handle of the putter more in the palms of both hands. In the left-hand putting grip (above) the club is placed diagonally from the base of the forefinger across the heel pad. The forefinger is off the shaft in the "reverse overlap" position, the thumb on top of the shaft. In the right-hand grip (right) the putter handle lies on a diagonal from the base of the forefinger to the heel pad, although in the completed grip it does not actually rest against that pad but rather against the middle finger of the left hand. The thumb is off the left side of the handle in the "harmless" position.

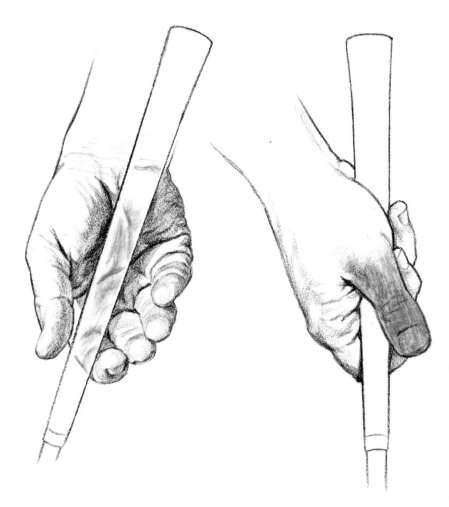

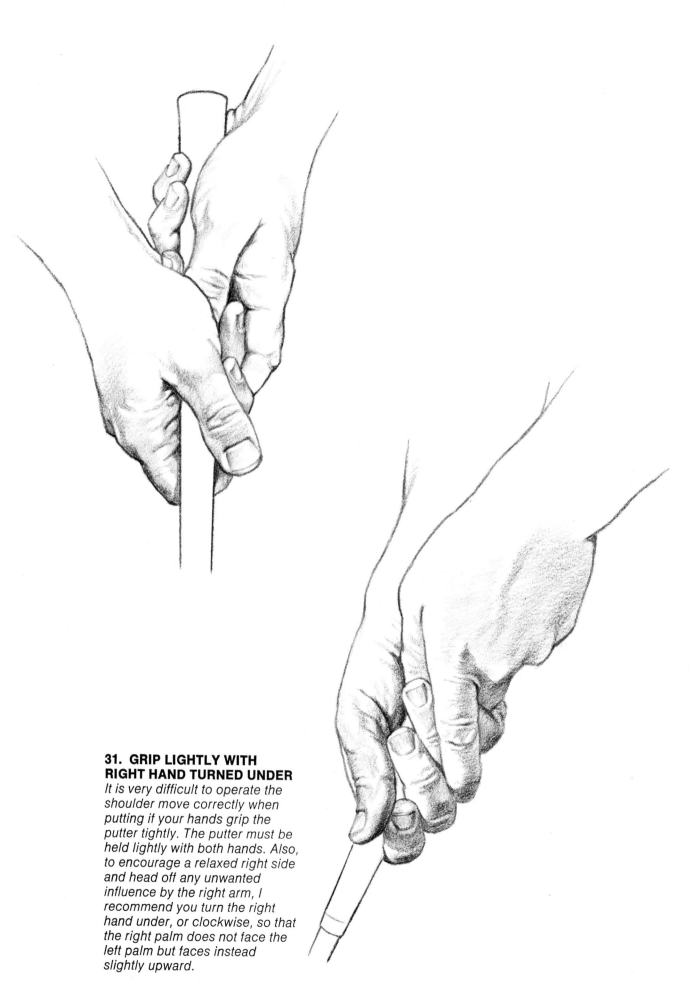

31. GRIP LIGHTLY WITH RIGHT HAND TURNED UNDER

It is very difficult to operate the shoulder move correctly when putting if your hands grip the putter tightly. The putter must be held lightly with both hands. Also, to encourage a relaxed right side and head off any unwanted influence by the right arm, I recommend you turn the right hand under, or clockwise, so that the right palm does not face the left palm but faces instead slightly upward.

forefinger, the ring finger of the right lying snugly against the middle finger of the left. The club runs diagonally up, across the palm, toward a spot just under the heel pad. However— and this is important—the club does not actually rest in the right palm. The fleshy part of your hand just under that heel pad should rest against the middle finger of your left hand.

Your right thumb should be in that harmless position off the left side of the shaft that I described for the full-shot grip, and in this case I mean *really* harmless. The right thumb should exert no influence whatsoever on the putting swing.

In contrast to the grip for full shots, the right palm does not face the left palm when you're putting. The right hand is turned slightly under, or clockwise. It's just a matter of a few degrees, but it serves to relax the right side. If the right hand is too high or square on the putter, it tends to tighten the muscles in the forearm and shoulders and it is in a position where it can be dominant. If you're concerned about this position causing you to close or otherwise alter the clubface during the swing, just keep in mind that the blade is being con— trolled by your shoulders, not by your hands (see illustration #31).

Again, *grip lightly* with both hands. It's impossible to operate the shoulder stroke effectively if your hands are holding the club firmly. The starting move is so small that the arms and hands will take over if they're exerting any pressure at all. So fondle the club . . . caress it. Don't worry about the swing being sloppy or the clubface opening and closing unnecessarily. The swing will remain on the right track because it is being moved by the shoulders.

Posture

The ideal putting posture is designed to eliminate tension. The lower body, therefore, should feel relaxed and normal. Flex your knees slightly but do not squat as on the full shot. This would create too much restriction and tension on the lower back. Your feet should be placed just far enough apart to maintain balance but not so far apart as to cause any tension in the hips or back. Because the putter is shorter than other clubs and because you want your arms to be relaxed and slightly bent, you should bend more than for a full swing (see illustration #32).

Let me caution you not to let your buttocks protrude too much to the rear. This makes you slouch. Keep your pelvis tucked under you a bit, giving you a position in which you can be firm and stable but still relaxed.

Aside from this more pronounced bend, the upper body attitude is much the same as for the full shot. Your lower back

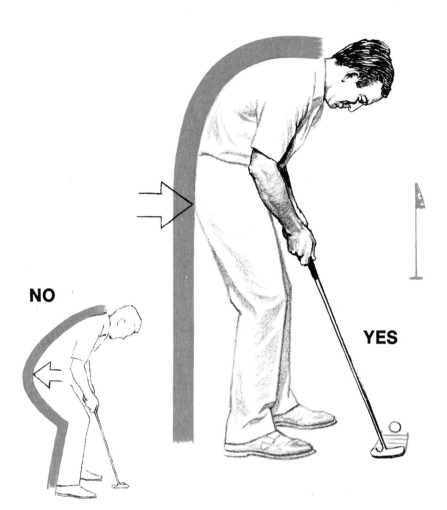

NO

YES

32. BEST PUTTING POSTURE ELIMINATES TENSION

The ideal putting posture eliminates tension, which enables you to make a correct start with the left shoulder. The knees should flex only slightly, just enough for comfort. The back is straight with buttocks tucked in. The shoulders are rounded with the chest caved in and relaxed. In this picture, the left shoulder has started turning, sending the putterhead back along the target path. The smaller illustration (left) shows improper putting posture; the knees are flexed too much, the buttocks are sagging to the rear. The back is not straight, the bend coming from the hips instead of the upper back area. This makes it difficult to start the left shoulder correctly.

is straight and you are round-shouldered, your chest caved in and relaxed. This posture eliminates all roadblocks to a free shoulder swing.

The arms remain relaxed and bent, hanging naturally. The inside of your right forearm should rest lightly against your right hip. The inside of your left forearm should brush your left side. If the arms were extended, it would be too easy to move them before you move your shoulders. Keep the hands close to the body so they can't become independent and jump the gun when you start.

There is not enough windup in the putting swing to make the forward stroke a reflexive action. So place the hands slightly ahead of the ball at address. The left hand should hang just inside the left thigh. The angle between the left forearm and the back of the left hand is much straighter than that of the right—in other words, the right wrist is more bent or hinged.

Remember always that your arms are relaxed, the hands holding the club lightly. If they are not, they'll take over the swing and the shoulder won't start.

The position you've now assumed—bent over correctly, arms hanging naturally and relaxed, hands comfortably close to the body rather than artificially extended—promotes a swing that tends to stay longer on the target path.

Alignment

The proper alignment of your shoulders for putting should be slightly left of a parallel to your target line. The reasons for this are basically the same as for a full shot. This induces a good shoulder turn because you feel you are turning onto the target line. Also, you can see and relate to the target line more clearly. That's why most good putters tend to address the ball a little open.

A warning, though—when we say *open,* we're talking about only fractions of inches in putting. The swing is too short and your shoulder turn too small to allow you to align as far left as you would for a full swing.

When your body is aligned to the right, in a closed position, you feel instinctively that you won't make a good shoulder turn because you're turning away from the target. That computer in your brain subconsciously tries to swing your body back toward the target. This brings the right side into play too soon and too disastrously.

Your feet, however, should be parallel to the target line rather than open. This is commonly called the square stance where a line across the toes runs parallel to the target line. If you get your right foot too far out past your left, you set up a roadblock in the clubhead path.

Ball Placement

In putting, the bottom of your swing arc will be in the center of your stance if you are doing everything properly. We want the putterface to contact the ball solidly while the blade is square and moving on line. So the ball should be placed at or just forward of the bottom of the swing arc, slightly left of center.

Most players position the ball too far forward, toward the left foot. This is fine for a full swing, in which your weight is moving forward and the bottom of your clubhead arc is elongated. But there is no such weight transference in putting. *Your putterhead follows a fixed path set by the movement of your shoulders.* It moves inside the line to down the line to back inside the line. If the ball is too far forward, your putterhead will pass the bottom of the arc and come inside before it gets to the ball. This results in clubface distortion and a cutting action that will pull the putt off line.

Target Projection

In putting, it is particularly important to keep your mind on the target, to visualize where you want the ball to go. That's because the target is so small—a cup 4¼ inches in diameter —and the stroke needed is so precise. Visualize the line on which you want the ball to roll into the hole and keep doing so while looking down in the direction of the ball. Or just think about a spot you can aim at on that target line. These thoughts will set in moton the instincts that will help you make the correct starting move.

Routine

A consistent, rhythmic routine is just as important in putting as it is on the full shot. First look at your target with your putter in your right hand. Place the putterhead down for a practice swing a few inches away from the ball. Align your feet and body as if you were going to stroke the putt. Take a practice swing or two. From this moment on, have only a picture of the target in your mind. Then move forward to the ball and place the putterhead squarely behind it. Maintain the same relative stance and body alignment. This becomes an automatic procedure that you shouldn't have to think about. Then let the shoulder start the swing.

Remember, you don't want to start a putt from a dead stop. It's easier to continue a motion than to originate one. So a smooth, continuous procedure, the backswing being activated by a target thought, will improve your chances of becoming a good putter.

The Stroke

The putting swing is less complicated and produces fewer surprises when you start it with your left shoulder. Remember that it is a *swing.* You must swing the shoulders to create enough momentum so that you don't have to hit with your right hand to supply power on the return (see illustration #33).

It's like singing a song. If you think of every word, every note, your song won't come out sounding right. By the same token, a putting stroke cannot be just a collection of notes. It must be a smooth harmony.

So go through your routine as I mentioned above, your upper body relaxed, think target and start the shoulder forward smoothly. Incidentally, there is no need for a forward press. If your body is properly relaxed the slightest thought will start the swing. There is no need to manufacture another move to get it going.

Moving the head is one of the major faults in putting. This usually is caused by taking the club back with the hands and arms, then supplying a right-side hit on the forward swing. The right shoulder moves the head forward. This destroys the alignment of the putter and changes the direction of its path.

Proper rotation of the shoulders corrects this problem

because the shoulders turn at right angles to the spine and create a stable axis. In putting, the spine is bent over more than on full shots, so the shoulders rotate in more of an up-and-down pattern. This means that when the left shoulder turns up on the forward swing, the right shoulder moves slightly down, underneath your head, instead of turning around and forcing the head forward.

When you no longer have to worry about that head movement, you can make a full, free follow-through. Obviously if you concentrate on keeping the head fixed, you will not follow through freely.

The shoulder turn establishes a correct axis, radius and plane. This also stabilizes the direction the putterhead travels because, so long as the shoulders control the swing, the axis, radius and plane won't vary. There is much less control with a hands-and-arms stroke.

You don't have to worry about keeping the putterhead low. It will stay low naturally. If you try to keep it low too far into the backswing you will pull the shoulder down, causing you to lose your axis and shut the blade. This starts your shoulders on an exaggerated up-and-down plane. Instead of returning the putter onto the target line, the left side pulls up too much and the putter moves up and away from the line.

The putterface stays square to the shoulders, not the target line. It will appear to stay square to that line on short putts but actually will open slightly on the backswing as the shoulders turn. It will do so even more on longer putts. So don't try to keep the putterhead going straight back too far from the ball. After the ball is struck, the putterhead will swing slightly inside the target line. This indicates the swing is being guided by the shoulders, not the hands. When you try to force the putterhead straight toward the target on the follow-through it places control in the hands (see illustration #34).

Here's something you cannot forget—*the longer the putt, the more turn you will need.* On a long putt, don't take the putter back the same distance as for a short putt, then try to accelerate more coming through. That will bring your right side into play. Or if you try to accelerate with your left side, your left hand and arm will move ahead of your body and disrupt your natural swing. So just go back farther, creating more windup and leverage. And don't forget that in putting as well as the full swing, *a good turn feels like no turn.*

Another important point to remember—the farther you swing the putter back on longer putts, the more your wrists will break. That's necessary to supply leverage. Centrifugal force created by the shoulder turn will take care of when or

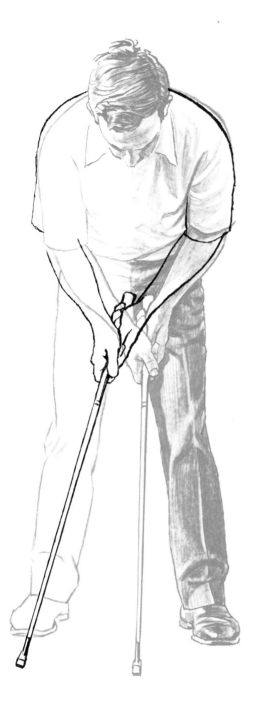

33. START PUTTING STROKE WITH LEFT SHOULDER

Because the putting stroke is so short, it takes only a slight movement of the shoulder to move the putterhead a considerable distance back along the target path, as indicated in this illustration. Initiating the putting stroke with the left shoulder places the stroke under the influence of the shoulders which makes the stroke much more stable than if it were controlled by the hands and arms. Remember that the putting stroke is a swing. If you have trouble starting your putting stroke correctly, a good practice thought is to imagine you have no right side to your body. This makes it easier for you to feel the starting move of the left shoulder and to sense the left side moving in control.

34. PUTTER FOLLOWS THE SHOULDERS, NOT TARGET LINE

On a proper forward swing, the putterface stays square to the shoulders, not the target line. The clubhead will move inside the target line after the ball is struck, indicating that the turning of the left shoulder rather than a manipulation with the hands is the propelling force. Trying to force the clubhead straight toward the target places control too much in the hands.

how much to hinge them. But don't try to restrict that wrist break. If you do, the ensuing lack of leverage will cause a lot of the mistakes we've talked about.

Earlier in this chapter I discussed the importance of practice swings in the short game. I want to reaffirm that, with a slightly different emphasis as far as putting is concerned.

In your practice swings preparatory to making the actual putt, you should be concerned with the feel of starting your shoulder. You should not consciously regulate the length of the stroke. But when you get ready to make the putt, *don't* think about mechanics. That would put the whole stroke under your conscious control, destroying its naturalness and inhibiting your touch and instinctive ability. So concentrate on starting the shoulder on the practice stroke, but think only of the target on the actual putt.

Never consciously think of distance and direction. Direction will be controlled by your mechanics. If you place the putterface down square to the line of flight and make a good swing, the putterface will return in that position. And distance, as I said earlier, comes from constant practice in hitting different putts of varying distances. If you try to control either of these factors consciously, you'll wreck the operation.

Some Tips On Reading Greens

The ability to judge a putting surface both for its speed and the amount of break or roll it will cause on a putt is vital to becoming a good putter. Much of this depends on practice and the development of your natural instincts, as I've said. But here are two suggestions which can help you improve faster:

● Look at the green as you're approaching it to get the general lay of the land. This will give you a better perspective of the slope of the green itself.

● Look at a putt from the side as well as the rear to give you a better idea of the contour. Sometimes a green slopes toward or away from you without your realizing it.

Exercises To Develop Putting Feel

● To recognize the feeling of the correct swing in putting, warm up by hitting a few long putts first. That gets you acquainted with the feeling of the left shoulder starting early. Then take progressively shorter putts, still remembering to start the left shoulder. On the very short putts the hands and arms will tend to take over and the shoulder might not move first. But having established the feeling of movement with the shoulder, you'll be able to recognize this and correct it.

● To improve your left-side control, pretend you have a line down the middle of your body and your right side doesn't exist. That means you have to swing solely with your left side. You'll be surprised at the immediate success you'll have with this thought. You'll feel as if you don't have a right side, but because your right side is much stronger and more coordinated, you're only balancing things.

CHAPTER SIX: HOW TO MAKE THE MOVE WORK ON THE COURSE

In this brief but very important chapter, I'm going to tell you why the move works where it really counts—on the golf course.

You are going to have anxiety at times, no matter how well you understand what you're doing. Tournament pressure, the bet with your Saturday foursome or just the thought of achieving a personal record score will take care of that. But because the one move I have given you sets up a series of reactions rather than a series of conscious actions, it gives you a swing that is much more dependable. Once you set it in motion you don't have to do anything. So you don't have to think about doing anything except starting the swing correctly. Therefore you are not so much at the mercy of your anxieties. Your swing is much more reliable than one based on *feel,* which can be affected to a much greater extent by changes in body chemistry, climate, temperature, humidity, fatigue, pressure, attitude and anxiety.

The method I've given you puts the golf swing in a neat package. It tells you what causes a good swing to happen at each step, why it happens and in what sequence. Once you've absorbed that, even when you hit a bad shot you're not going to ask yourself, "What did I do and what am I going to do now?" You can go back to the method and say, "Well, if I hit from the top, I either did this, this or this wrong." And since you have a clear path to your goals, you will have less trouble monitoring your anxiety and keeping it under control. You will put yourself in a psychological state to perform efficiently.

The psychology of golf is more important than the mechanics of the swing. I see many good players with bad swings but relaxed, confident attitudes that let them get the last ounce of effectiveness out of their swings. On the other hand, there are players with pretty good moves who never become proficient because they lack confidence, have negative attitudes and are constantly making mechanical changes that they feel will help them. But they never trust those changes when an important shot looms so they are seldom able to produce under pressure.

The one move I have presented to you and its inevitable results give you, I believe, a solid foundation for successful play. In fact, I think it will improve your game if you only believe in it a little. But even this move cannot bring you to your fullest potential without a confident, positive approach on your part.

That's why I've been so careful to explain all that happens and what is accomplished when you make the one move.

Without the total picture in your mind, you might concentrate so intently on starting the left shoulder that you would increase tension. That's the last thing you want to happen. As I have stressed, you can't make the move well and make this method work if you're not relaxed. And you can't relax if you have some anxiety about how it's going to work.

You must be able to monitor your anxiety level and know what causes that anxiety, if you're going to overcome it. The average player gets anxious because he doesn't understand what's going on in a golf swing. He doesn't have a logical sequence of events that fits into a neat parcel, with all the pieces intact. So his level of anxiety is the result of shock treatments over a period of time. Sure, he hits good shots once in a while, but all of a sudden something goes wrong and he doesn't know what it is. He might find the answer, he might hit a shot that goes straight, but then he loses it again. Since he really doesn't know what he's doing he keeps grabbing at quick cures, and when they fail him his level of anxiety goes even higher.

Actually, I suspect millions of players are helped through a better functioning of the left shoulder without knowing it. Having accepted a gimmick cure, even temporarily, a player tends to reduce his anxiety level and so becomes more relaxed. This usually makes the upper left side move better instinctively. But because the gimmick wasn't sound, he's soon back where he started, groping from one area of confusion to another. By contrast, with the method in this book, you're in full command of the whole process.

For example, a conscious thrusting with the legs at the start of the forward swing can only happen through a decision to move, which is more at the mercy of your emotional ups and downs. When you're on the practice tee and the shot doesn't mean anything, you can do it. When you're relaxed, you get cooperation from your body and it carries you through.

But under the rigors of competition, when you're leading the tournament as a pro, one under par as an amateur or about to win the eighth flight title at your club, your body tightens and you get a lot of static in your mind which raises that anxiety level. Then a conscious act doesn't work as efficiently as an automatic response, and the conscious leg drive gives way to the stronger impulse to hit with the right side from the top of the swing.

By starting that left shoulder early, however, you have immediately established a position of leverage and put your shoulders enough under the influence of the centrifugal force of club, arms and hands to give your left side the advantage. You've set it up for your left leg to go first no matter how nervous you are . . . and it will.

When you play, you can't pull the golf swing apart. You can't take too many thoughts to the golf course and expect your swing to work. There is too much going on out there to be concerned with all the parts, especially when pressure is on. Thinking about one movement simplifies the whole thing.

For one thing, it makes the swing more consistent on the course. When you're on the practice tee, the feel of the last shot is fresh in your mind and it's easy to repeat the swing. On the course you must wait several minutes between shots. Having only one move to consider each time helps you produce a better swing more often.

It also helps you focus your mind on how to execute the shot rather than the *meaning* of it. Concentrating on results, what the shot can mean to you, builds the anxiety which inhibits automatic reaction. But if you have just one simple mechanical procedure to trigger the swing, you are more apt to focus your attention on that and away from distracting thoughts. This lowers your anxiety, allows you to relax and lets you make the move better.

As important as anything is the fact that having only this move to consider allows your instincts to take over. There are many physical actions you can do better subconsciously than consciously. This is proved by the way we walk. If you tried to make your steps exactly the same length each time, they would vary. But if you walk naturally, your steps tend to be the same.

I once read of an experiment in which a man was directed to brush his teeth each day and chart how he made the motions. Motion pictures showed that each day he did it differently. Yet when motion pictures were taken of him when he wasn't thinking about brushing his teeth, he did it the same way every time.

The scientists conducting these experiments concluded that certain mechanical movements, motion skills involving muscle memory, are much more easily and consistently done by your subconscious.

Tempo or swing speed is an example that I touched on earlier. Your swing tempo is much more consistent, natural and coordinated when you don't think about it.

When you throw a ball to somebody or pitch a penny, you don't think about how hard to throw it. You have learned that motor skill. So you look at the target, which transmits an impulse to your mind, and invariably you throw the ball or penny the right distance. The same principle applies in golf. After you've learned to hit various golf shots, been on the practice tee and played some golf, your instincts will tell you how hard to hit the ball. Your conscious mind is free to consider only where you want it to go and one thing to do to start it on its way.

Practice helps, of course, and the more you do of it the better you'll play. But you don't need a great deal of practice to see improvement. Your progress will be quickest if you do not allow yourself to be diverted by trying something else that may or may not work.

Now I'm going to give you some practical and specific tips that will help you make the move on the course. The golfer who makes a relaxed, beautifully coordinated practice swing at an imaginary ball, or even the one who is swinging smoothly on the practice tee, usually becomes a totally different animal on the golf course.

In the first place, the instinct to hit *at* the ball and propel it to a particular spot, to make a particular score, to win a bet, to win a tournament, to gain esteem in the eyes of his fellow players often causes anxieties and extraneous thoughts that hinder the ability to make a good starting move with the upper left side.

Add to this the dissatisfaction or occasional temper flare-up when a shot or two goes awry, plus the normal problem of maintaining an efficient level of concentration for a period of three or four hours.

The secret of successful play is to develop and maintain the proper mental atitude toward playing each individual shot and the round in its entirety so you can retain the equanimity and relaxed attitude you need to perform the move well for 18 holes.

What follows in this final chapter is a compendium of thoughts which will help you do this. These suggestions will keep your mind more at ease and your body more relaxed, better enabling you to use the one starting move to better golf.

ON PRACTICING

The method I've given you in this book doesn't require a lot of practice at one time. You're better off practicing a few minutes each day, or however often you can, rather than going out for a block-buster three-hour session once a week. That's because this concept stresses relaxation of the mind and subsequently relaxation of the muscles to make them work. If you stand out there beating balls for hours, you'll become mentally and physically fatigued. Your muscles will get tighter and you are liable to get sluggish, hindering the relaxed action that starts your upper left side.

If you're having problems, practice with the clubs that are easiest for you to handle. Generally, these are the short irons. Try a 7-iron, which is long enough to require a good motion but short enough that you won't try to hit it hard. A few successful short-iron shots will breed relaxation and enable you to start that left shoulder earlier.

I feel that in any well-organized half-hour practice session, only five minutes should be spent hitting woods. Your swing will become better grooved with the shorter clubs, and success with the woods will follow.

ON WARMING UP

When you are warming up before a round, do just that. Don't confuse warming up with practicing. Decide on a certain number of shots to hit . . . for example, four with a wedge, four with a 7-iron, four with a 5-iron, four with the 2-iron, four with the driver. Then stick with this formula, no matter how well or badly you hit the ball. All you're trying to do is loosen up.

If you hit the ball badly on the practice tee and start trying to correct a fault you will approach your round in a negative frame of mind. By hitting just a prearranged number of shots, even if they go badly, you won't get tense. Furthermore, you won't lose confidence on the practice tee and you will go to the first tee in a more relaxed frame of mind. This will better enable you to start the swing correctly with the left shoulder.

ON MAKING PRACTICE SWINGS

I don't advocate making practice swings during actual play, except on short shots and putts for the reasons I explained in Chapter 5. In the first place, a full practice swing causes fatigue, both immediately and during the course of a round. It takes your muscles several seconds to recover from activity. If you take a hard practice swing and immediately step up to the ball, you will be making your regular swing with your muscles in a state of lesser efficiency. And if you take a practice swing or two before every full shot, you will be swinging two or three times more than the player who doesn't. By the time you reach the last few holes, you'll be tired and you will have difficulty making a good left shoulder move. Too many practice swings can hinder proper relaxation.

ON HITTING SPECIAL SHOTS

Situations on the course often demand that you bend the shape of your shots. Sometimes you must fade or slice the ball (move it from left to right) and sometimes you must intentionally draw or hook it (from right to left). In trying to bend shots, or hit the ball higher or lower than normal, it is not necessary to change your starting move or to violate the four swing fundamentals. All I do is build the fade or draw into my address position.

To draw or hook the ball—you can achieve a right-to-left pattern in your shots by using a stronger grip, moving your hands clockwise so that more left-hand knuckles are showing at address. I prefer to do this by setting the club down so that the face is slightly closed and then assume my normal grip. Then I square the clubface, making sure that I don't change my grip as I turn the club. This is just an easy way to move your hands over on the shaft in the so-called strong position. It buffers this change, making you less self-conscious of it. This creates less interference in making a normal move with the left shoulder. The stronger hand position insures that the club will roll and close more in the impact area.

And remember, if you are drawing or hooking a shot, you must aim and align a spot to the right of your primary target.

To fade or slice the ball—I prefer to move the hands left, or counterclockwise, on the club, aim slightly left and let the ball fade back onto the target. If I want a big slice, I open the stance a little more. Again, to combat the change in feel that occurs by moving the hands left, or weaker, I take my grip the same way as for a sand shot. I open the clubface slightly and place my hands on the grip in the normal fashion. I then turn the club (counterclockwise) until the face is square, without changing my hands. The hands are now more to the left than normal, but I've buffered the change in feel by placing them on the club the way I'm used to. As I have mentioned, this is less apt to change the feel at address or interfere with the left shoulder start.

To hit low shots—this one is easy. Simply move the ball back in your stance so you'll be striking it just before the clubhead reaches the bottom of its arc. This de-lofts the clubface and thus the ball will fly lower. The farther back you get the ball, the lower it's going to fly. It will help you in hitting low shots if you take one club longer than you would ordinarily and simply choke down on the grip and make a shorter swing.

To hit high shots—play the ball farther forward so the clubhead actually is ahead of the hands at address. Be careful not to get so far ahead you have to make an unnatural move to get to it. You also may find it helpful to open the clubface a bit. You'll have to aim slightly to the left, because the shot will fade, but it will get up quickly. Try to stay behind the ball a little longer than normal with your upper body in the forward swing. Target projection helps here, and you'll also find it valuable to look at the object you are trying to clear, or at a cloud . . . this will encourage the proper instincts.

In the case of both the high and low shots, I suggest that no basic changes in your approach to the swing be made so that the start with your upper left side will be as natural and instinctive as always.

ON PLAYING WITH EASE

Perhaps you've heard the expression "play within yourself." That simply means you don't hit every shot as hard as you can, and it may be the best advice I or anyone can give you.

It's been my experience that every time a middle- or high-handicap player—and sometimes a low-handicapper —reaches into his bag, he pulls out a club that he must hit perfectly to reach the target. The game is difficult enough without placing that added burden on yourself. Instead, why not pick out a club that you can mis-hit slightly, that you can swing with someting less than an all-out effort?

Knowing that you have a little extra club in your hand, that you don't have to swing full tilt, will produce some immediate benefits. It will create relaxation of the upper body, which will allow you to effectively start the left shoulder. Because this improves your rhythm and timing at the same time, you undoubtedly will hit the ball farther than ever. For years I've seen golfers hit their longest shots when they're swinging easily, for those very reasons. Conversely, swinging hard will make it almost impossible to start the swing correctly with the left shoulder.

All you have to do is start the left shoulder in a relaxed manner and you'll get all the distance you need.

This will also conserve your strength. It's like a baseball pitcher who throws every pitch as hard as he can . . . pretty soon he tires and loses control. Or a batter who goes for the home run every time. He may get a few, but he's going to strike out a lot, too.

That's why you'll be the victim of erratic shots by the time you get to the back nine if you try to hit a home run every time. The good player, the professional who does it for a living, learns to swing with three-quarters effort. If he doesn't, if he hits a full shot all the time, eventually he'll start to make some right-sided swings and lose control.

By swinging easy, I don't necessarily mean swinging slower or softer. I'd rather see you choke down on the club an inch or two and make a shorter swing. That's the best mechanical process.

To be able to hit the ball easily, it's important that you know how far you hit each club. To determine this, simply take a club—say a 7-iron—and hit 25 or 30 shots under normal conditions in an area where you can measure the results. Measure the longest and the shortest and the in-between and strike an average.

Bear in mind that it's easy to overpower the short irons and hit them for distances out of proportion to the rest of your clubs. So make sure you're not doing this when you compute your ranges.

Once you've learned your distances, club selection becomes easier. For example, I hit a 7-iron between 145 and 155 yards. I always find it better to concentrate on the short or "easy" end of my range. When I get to 155 yards, I often take a 6-iron, because that's at the easy end of its range. Remember, there are no prizes for hitting an 8-iron where somebody else is hitting a 7-iron. On the other hand, your ability to better start the left shoulder with the longer club when you're more relaxed is a valuable prize indeed.

ON PICKING THE RIGHT CLUB

On those occasions when you're not sure how far it is to your target, I find it's best to trust your first instincts. Once you have some experience on the course, the first glance at your target forms a picture of your shot. The thought of a club will cross your mind. It's almost always best to go with that thought. Even if it's the wrong club you'll probably hit a better shot than if you let yourself get tied up by indecision. That can only hinder the early starting of your left shoulder and cause you to make a poor swing.

Because this picture of the shot and the correct club forms instinctively, don't look at the target until it's time to play. You might measure the distance, if there's a yardage indicator in the vicinity, but wait until you're ready to hit the shot to look at the target, evaluate the wind and other conditions, and get that picture in your mind. Then, without giving yourself time to let negative thoughts encroach, pick the club that impulse tells you is right and hit the shot.

ON HITTING THE BALL HARD

Despite what I said earlier about striking your shots with three-quarter effort, there are certain times when you must hit the ball harder and farther than normal. This usually is with the driver, but sometimes it's with an iron which you must use to get over a tree or other hazard and still carry a greater-than-normal distance.

Simply knowing you have to hit the ball harder will program your mind to speed up your arm swing. The secret then is to get in the proper position to allow yourself to do this. So don't stand there and work yourself up to hit the ball farther. That will just tighten your upper body muscles and force you to hit more with your right side. You'll hit it shorter, if anything. Just try to be relaxed and graceful and soft in your upper body. I think you'll be amazed at how far you can carry the ball this way.

I find another trick that helps in tight situations is to concentrate on the hazard you must carry—water, a bunker, whatever it is. It is better to face the problem directly. This eases the pressure because you are concentrating on overcoming the problem, not trying to mentally avoid it. As a result, you are much better able to relax.

ON PLAYING FROM HEAVY ROUGH

In thick rough the grass usually gets between the ball and the club. It also wraps around the hosel of the club, twisting the clubface into a closed position at impact which makes it very difficult to get the ball out. Even if you do get out, that intervening grass will take most of the spin off the ball and make it difficult to control. That's why I recommend that the average player never take less than a 5-iron to escape from the rough. With any less-lofted club, he risks leaving the ball in just as tough a position as before.

The higher-lofted woods that are becoming popular are helpful in play from heavy grass. The 7-wood especially can be helpful. Because it slides through the grass more easily, it's often a better tool than an iron.

Another benefit of selecting these longer clubs is that you instinctively realize you will be able to escape without placing strain on your swing. This relaxes you and makes that good, early move with the left shoulder easier to achieve.

ON COMPETING IN THE RAIN

Many—perhaps most—players rely on "feel," which is quickly distorted in foul weather. Moisture causes slippery grips, extra clothing, difficulty in judging distance and other distractions. But if your swing depends to a great extent on simply starting that left shoulder early and well, feel is much less a factor. You'll be more able to maintain your playing equilibrium in the rain.

One tip for playing in wet weather—use more lofted wood clubs in the fairway. For example, use a 4-wood where a 3-wood might normally be required. Water will tend to get between the clubface and the ball and act as grass does in the same situation, lessening the spin you can achieve. This makes the 4-wood act like a 3-wood. With the irons, however, you may get the opposite effect. They may cut too deeply into the soft turf so you'll need more club, and perhaps a shorter, easier swing to maintain balance and club control.

ON TEEING THE BALL

Tee the ball on the left side of the teeing area whenever possible. It gives you the feeling of swinging out to your target and programs a better starting move with the left shoulder and induces a left-sided forward swing. If you tee the ball in the middle or on the right side of the teeing ground, it's easy to get the feeling that you are turning too much away from your target. This instinctively will hinder the good move with your left shoulder. It also tends to make you swing *around* to get the ball into the middle of the fairway, thus encouraging too much right-side activity.

ON PLAYING WITH SLUGGERS

If you're playing with a golfer who drives the ball much farther than you do, try not to watch him. If you do, there might be an unconscious tendency to press on your own drive, and this usually is fatal to starting the left shoulder early and well. Remember, golf is an individual game of skill, not a contest of strength.

ON PLAYING WITH YOUR TENDENCIES

If you're hitting the ball a certain way, even if it's not the way you'd like, don't try to change during a round. Hasty repair work on the course can only heighten your anxiety and increase muscle tension so you just get worse. Instead, remember that the success of your golf swing depends on how immediate your left shoulder turn is.

So relax, think about making the good start with your shoulder and don't fight your tendencies. Allow for them. That attitude in itself might straighten you out.

For example, if you're hitting the ball to the right, aim to the left. That way you won't be trying to keep the ball from going right, which is probably what is causing your problem in the first place.

Think back to a day when you might have been consistently slicing the ball. Suddenly you come to a hole that doglegs right and you figure your slice will be welcome. But the ball goes straight! The reason is that you were willing to let the ball slice, so you didn't try to stop it . . . which means you didn't activate your right side in an attempt to pull the ball around. Instead you made a better swing and produced a straight shot.

By the same token, if you're having a lot of problems with a particular shot, look for a suitable alternative. If your wedge play is shaky, for instance, don't be ashamed to use your putter if at all possible, no matter how far off the green you might be. A professional-looking shot doesn't pay any more dividends, particularly if you miss every other one. Getting the ball close to or in the cup by any method is what counts.

Finally, apply the same philosophy to wind play. Don't fight a stiff breeze. If it's blowing right to left, allow for it. If it's in your face, don't try to hit the ball harder. Hit it easier, in fact. For the reasons I mentioned earlier, you'll relax, start the upper left side earlier and hit the ball farther than if you're pressing.

ON COUNTING YOUR BLESSINGS

Golf is a frustrating, humbling game, perhaps the most difficult sport in which to excel. Because it represents such a challenge, because it is so easy to transform a good hole into a triple bogey or a good round into a disaster, golf can cause a great loss of composure, even cause irrationality. I've seen persons well-adjusted in their business and personal lives who are driven to the depths by a missed shot or a bad hole. They feel helpless and useless and they might as well walk off the course right then, because their round is over and they're certainly not going to get any pleasure out of the rest of it.

That's too bad, because it really is only a game for most players, one which can be enjoyed whether you shoot par or 140. I've found that an effective antidote to the tension caused by a missed shot is putting everything in its proper perspective. Remind yourself that you've got your health, a nice family, a good job, a nice home . . . breathe the fresh air, smell a flower or two, feel the warm sunshine, and remember that however badly you're doing at the moment, it sure beats working. Besides, there is always tomorrow.

If you do that, you'll be more apt to approach the next shot with a clear head and a positive attitude. This will relax you and allow you to make a good starting move. And while this may sound more like psychology than golf instruction, I think you're beginning to realize the importance of the mental approach in this game.

ON PLANNING YOUR SHOTS

You should have a target for every shot, including your tee shot. As I explained in Chapter 4, target projection gives you something to trigger your swing. There should be a reason for picking your target, a reason why you want to hit the ball where you do. To determine this, plan each hole in advance. Figure the best angle from which to approach the green— if the flag is left, you'll probably want to come in from the right, for example. To set up the best approach, then, you'll have to decide which side of the fairway to hit your drive, or your second shot on a par-5.

In other words, don't just launch the ball into the blue without a plan or you will pay for it in wasted shots. Having a blueprint for each hole breeds confidence that lets you relax, make the good move and produce shots that are not only well struck but effectively placed.

ON ACCEPTING MISSED SHOTS

One important thing to keep in mind is that it's not your perfect shots but your *good misses* that help you score consistently well in golf. If you'll honestly analyze your game, you'll discover that you hit almost no perfect shots, a few very good ones and the rest of them down the scale from there. You're no different than Bobby Jones, Ben Hogan, Jack Nicklaus or any other star in that respect. Almost every shot you hit is a miss, measured against the standard of perfection. Your goal, then, is to keep that degree of miss to a minimum so the shot still will be serviceable, still will wind up on the fairway, somewhere on or close to the green.

The good players do this, and if you'll approach your game from this standpoint, you'll be much more relaxed and better prepared mentally to live with your mis-hits. You can concentrate instead on starting the left shoulder early and making the lowest score possible. If your best shots become the standard you expect, rather than your goal, you're in for a lot of frustration.

This advice is particularly good in bad weather or when you're tired. Accept the fact that you'll be likely to mis-hit more shots, particularly if you start trying too hard. Concentrate on taking more club and not getting upset by your mishaps. In the end, you can turn misadventure into triumph.

ON GAMBLING

For most of us, a decision on whether to gamble or hit a safe shot must be made several times a round. Usually we'll have to play our next shot from across a long carry over water. What to do? You must, of course, make a positive decision one way or the other. This breeds the confidence and peace of mind that lets you make the relaxed, early move with the left shoulder. Indecision only throws up roadblocks that hinder this move.

To decide whether or not to gamble, ask yourself two questions and answer them honestly. The first is, *Do I have a pretty good chance of pulling it off or are the odds against me?* This involves knowing your own capabilities, plus being realistic about the situation. If you really think that a shot from behind trees to the green would demand a miracle to be successful—and assuming you don't need such a miracle to win your match or the tournament—then you're better off in the long run choosing the safest route to the fairway. A bogey is better than a large number, and you still may have a chance to make a good shot and putt for a par.

If you decide the odds are in your favor, then take the gamble . . . if you can answer the second question. *Does the result warrant a gamble?* In other words, with a successful gamble you should have a very good chance of saving a shot or two.

For example, if a tee shot between a lake and an out-of-bounds will get you 30 yards from the green, whereas a safe 4-wood would leave you 80 yards away, don't gamble. It's about as tough to get down in two from 30 yards as it is from 80 or 100. The over-all odds favor playing it safe. On the other hand, if threading the needle through trees can get you 10 yards from the green or closer and a safe chip to the fairway leaves you 60 yards out, you ought to go for it. My criterion is whether the gamble gets you on the green or very close to the hole.

There are times, of course, that the circumstances dictate

a gamble, even against the odds. If the tournament or the match hangs on a risky shot, by all means gamble. You really have nothing to lose. But most of the time you'll be better off abiding by the guidelines I've given you.

Another factor in your decision to gamble or not is the level of your golfing skill. By this I mean, if you're striking the ball consistently well, go ahead and risk the shot down the right side of the fairway where the out-of-bounds stakes lurk if it will get you a better second-shot angle into the green. If you're a good bunker player, a good pitcher and chipper of the ball, I feel it's an advantage to attack the course. Go ahead and throw the ball at the pin directly over a trap. If you miss, you'll be able to recover.

If you have the game to back you up, you can go on the offensive with your shots. The importance of this is that it perpetuates an aggressive attitude that helps you make the left shoulder move better. If you are timid, you're less likely to do it as confidently and well. It also gets you used to playing these kinds of shots, of taking the considered gamble, so that you can rely on making the move better when the time comes that you really have to take a chance.

I've noticed a lot of players with good golf games who play conservatively most of the time. Then, when a situation arises in which they have a gamble, they're not ready for it. They succumb to the pressure and miss the shot. They have to change their attitude from defense to offense, and there aren't many around who can do that on a moment's notice.

ON PLAYING TOUGH

Golf, successfully played, is not for the weak-minded. It's a game for the tough-minded optimist. I've seen bad golf swings work because the player was that sort . . . never dwelled on his mistakes, never worried about whether he was going to strike the golf ball well, even if his previous performance that day didn't warrant optimism. He stayed 100 per cent positive.

That kind of attitude will help you start the left shoulder early and effectively. It can help you achieve your fullest potential within the limits of your physical capabilities and the time and effort you can devote to the game.

The most important idea I can leave with you is never let a negative thought enter your mind when you're playing golf. You want to be 100 per cent positive in your approach to every shot. This is just as important as having a sound swing . . . maybe more so. If you feel your alignment is wrong, your grip position not just right or the club in your hand is the wrong one, you're more likely to miss the shot because subconscious doubt will interfere with starting your upper left side. You'd better back off and readjust your thinking before you try again.

If you've just missed 10 shots in a row, try approaching the 11th as if you've hit 10 in a row perfectly. This can help you build the image and confidence you need to let the left shoulder move work well.

What is success in golf? For some it's a 35 handicap, for some to break 100 or 90, for some to break par. The instant you make that number, the number changes. That's the fascination of the game—you always think you're about to find the secret. Some days you do, and then it's gone again. When you become as good as you wanted to be, you then want to be better. The thing that makes this the greatest game in the world is that you can be.

One thing I know . . . and want you to believe—the method and the thoughts you have been given in this book will make you better prepared to search for and find that elusive grail.